DO IT YOURSELF PUBLISHING
~ CHEAP & EASY

A step-by-step guide to

Independent Publishing

for authors

I0428572

By Indie Published Author
J Monkeys

Copyright © 2014 Jennifer Moncuse
January 2014

ISBN: 1475017626
ISBN 13: 978-1475017625

For more information about author J Monkeys, see www.jmonkeys.com.

Other books by J Monkeys:

Questions for Preschoolers (photographs & questions for preschoolers)
> In the Woods
> Street Sign Scavenger Hunt

Dixie & Taco's Adventures (for parents to read with kindergartners)
> Dixie & Taco go to Grandmother's House
> Dixie & Taco go to Grandmother's House (English & Spanish)
> Dixie & Taco go to the Zoo
> Dixie & Taco go to the Beach

First Grade Readers (for 1st Graders to read on their own)
> Brook the Fish

The Livingston-Wexford Adventures (a 'tween paranormal series)
> The Cordovan Vault
> The Peacock Tale

Non-Fiction
> DIY Publishing ~ Cheap & Easy
> DIY Publishing ~ Cheap & Easy Companion

Table of Contents

Table of Tables

ACKNOWLEDGEMENTS

Fusco and Pope: Thanks for your help! I appreciate it.

Haertel: What can I say? You're a treasure!

Hubby Extraordinaire: Thanks for the willingness to eat pizza when I forgot to make dinner again, for putting the kids to bed after a long day at work so I could write, and for being an all-around wonderful guy.

About this Book

I am not a copyright lawyer

This book is intended to help you make your "original works of authorship" available to others to read. "Original works of authorship" is a term from the 1976 US Copyright Act which provides legal protection against plagiarism, or the theft of your work. I am not an Intellectual Property Rights Lawyer and the advice in this book should not be understood as such. If what you are interested in publishing *isn't* an original work of authorship, then you should seek competent advice on the legalities of publishing it. In no way is this book advocating plagiarism.

I am an Independently Published author.

The steps outlined in this book will help you to become an Independently Published author, too. I'm assuming that if you are buying this book, you've already written a book yourself and you want to publish it.

Visual Aids

I've added some symbols to this book to tell you a few things at a glance.

$ This icon is an indication that this topic is one where you may need to spend some money. In these areas, I offer suggestions on how you can accomplish the goal on the cheap.

⟨X⟩ This icon is an indication that the topic discussed here is a specific step for you to do. You may want to open up your computer and try it with the book next to you, or you might want to flag the page for future reference.

This icon is an indication that there's an idea here to help you if you get stuck. You might want to flag it for future reference, or highlight it.

Checklists

There are checklists at the end of the book to recap the steps you need to take to publish your book. The checklists are also available together in a companion workbook. See www.jmonkeys.com for more information.

Chapter 1: Indie Publishing 101

What do I know about Indie Publishing?

Hey, that's a great question! Why on earth should you take my advice? Well, I am an Indie Published author. As J Monkeys (my pen name for people under eighteen) I've Indie Published eight books. And I'm writing this handbook while I'm publishing one, so the information is real-time. These are the steps and tools I use to publish and market my books.

What is Indie Publishing?

Independent Publishing is so new that there isn't one definition that is truly accepted by everybody yet. But think about Indie Film. People have a sense of what an Indie Movie is. These are the movies made by independent filmmakers but *outside* of the major studios.

The Indie Publishing definition I'm going with here is: **a book published *outside* of the traditional publishing houses.**

So what does it mean to be Indie Published? This is not the same thing as the old Vanity Press where an author would pay $20,000 and end up with a garage full of copies of their book. Nor is it something just for folks whose book isn't good enough for Traditional Publishing which is what people often think of when they hear the term "Self-Published." Being Indie Published isn't "less" than being Traditionally Published. And yes, an Indie Published book is a "real" book.

Is Indie Publishing Right for You?

There are a lot of factors to consider when determining which approach is right for you. Chances are, you've already given the Indie route some thought since you bought this book, but in case you aren't sure, Table 1.1 is my Indie Pub vs. Traditional Pub comparison.

Table 1.1 Indie vs. Traditional

Topic	Indie Pub	Traditional Pub
Editing your Manuscript	You need to find your own resource to polish your manuscript.	The publisher has people to take your final draft, request content changes, sometimes substantial ones, and polish it up.
Book Title	Author chooses the title.	Author has little to no input into title.
Cover Art	Author will do it or pay someone out of his/her pocket.	Author has limited input into cover art; the publisher picks it and pays for it.
Printing Books	Author pays for print copies, but it's cheap.	Publisher pays to have the books printed.
Testimonials	Author finds them.	Publisher may be able to get them for you.
Reviews	Author finds reviewers.	Publisher will be able to get them for you.
Press Release	Author will write and send out press release.	Marketing department will take care of it.
Marketing	Author is solely responsible for marketing.	Author is largely responsible for marketing.
Timing of Release	Author can release books whenever desired.	Author has no input and it could/will easily be two years out.
Money	Author gets no advance but earns much larger royalty rates (85% for some e-books) for the length of copyright instead of just however long the book is available for sale.	New authors get small, if any advance and need to earn it back before any royalties are paid. Royalty rates are in the range of 14% (and I've heard lower, like 8%) for as long as the publisher sells the books.

For me, the gray highlighted items were the issues that led me down the Indie Publishing path. For my first book, *The Cordovan Vault*, the title and the look of the book were very important to me. I didn't like the idea of someone changing those things.

I also really didn't want to wait two years to see my name on the spine of a book. It took me seven years to finish writing the thing, and I just didn't want to wait another pair of years, at least. Publishers are working several years out and they have to fit new books into their catalog. It takes time.

The real clincher, though, was the **Marketing/Money** balance. Debut authors rarely bring in big advances, with a few very well-known exceptions. There doesn't seem to be an "average" advance. I've heard that folks get something like $5,000 – $10,000 for a debut romance, but you can't get your book looked at without an agent and agents say they don't represent anything that will bring in less than a $10,000 advance. That likely varies by genre.

Let's look at an example of a good deal for a first time author: a three-book deal.

> An author is offered $30,000 dollars for three books, 15% of which goes to the agent, and the remaining amount ($25,500) comes to the author as he hits specific benchmarks.
>
> - $4,250 when he signs the contract. (Now.)
> - $4,250 when the final version of book 1 is accepted. (Likely several months from now.)
> - $4,250 when the concept for book 2 is accepted. (Likely sometime after book one is finalized – maybe 8-12 months from now.)
> - $4,250 when the final version of book 2 is accepted. (Likely 18 months from now.)

- $4,250 when the concept for book 3 is accepted. (Likely 24 months from now, about the same time that book 1 is heading to the bookstore.)
- $4,250 when the final version of book 3 is accepted. (Likely 30 months from now.)

Of course, the payments can be contracted in any number of ways and the agent probably won't get all their money up front, but as a part of each payment from the publisher to the author.

The other part of the Marketing/Money balance is the fact that debut authors don't get much love when it comes to marketing. The author is going to have to do almost all of the heavy lifting alone.

Agents

Now, I want to take a minute to say a little something about agents (Literary Agents). In the post 9-11 world, publishers don't go through the slush pile the way they used to back in the 1970's and 80's. The "slush pile" is the mountain of unsolicited manuscripts that arrive on publishers' doorsteps every day via the US mail. Many publishers' websites now say they don't accept slush and it gets returned to sender, or destroyed without ever being opened. They only accept submissions from agents.

Agents are in the business of knowing who's buying what. A good agent can get an author much more advance money than an unagented author, but getting an agent can be as big of a time-consuming challenge as getting a publisher to buy your book.

Being traditionally published does mean that you are likely to be on the shelf at Barnes & Noble, at least for a little while. Go the Indie route and you won't be in B&N (at least not right now) although they'll sell you on their website.

Sales Venues & Royalties

But being traditionally published also means that you have to play by their rules when it comes to building an audience. Meaning, you'd better build it fast, because shelf space in the sole big-chain national bookstore is at a premium and they don't keep books that don't sell in that prime space. Books get sent back to the distributor, often within weeks of release.

The advance that traditionally published authors get is an Advance on Royalties. You have to earn that back (at your royalty rate of pennies on the dollar) before you earn any additional money from your book. And the publishing house determines how long the book is available for purchase (how long it's in print). If the book isn't available for sale, you aren't going to earn anything more.

Being Indie Published, I decide when to take my books out of print or when to stop making them available for purchase. And I have time on my side to make more money than that four-figure advance I likely would have gotten. Copyright law gives me seventy years after I die before my work goes into the public domain and I (or my heirs) stop earning money from it.

Role Models

HP Mallory and Amanda Hocking are two extremely successful authors who started out by Indie Publishing their books. They both sold LOTS of books this way. Like hundreds of thousands of copies. In Hocking's case – reportedly millions of copies of her books have been sold. And perhaps you've heard of a little book called *Fifty Shades of Grey* by EL James. That was originally an Indie Published book, too. Of course, they are unusually successful. But it's something to consider.

Here's the math that convinced me. I'm forty years old and pretty healthy. Let's say I live another forty years, and add to that my seventy years of copyright, for a total of one hundred ten "earning" years. I only have to earn $182 a year from *The Cordovan Vault* to make $20,000, or double what I might have gotten in advance from a traditional publisher. And I think I'm going to do a whole lot better than that.

Now it's time for you to decide which route is the right one for you.

- **Traditional Publishing** may mean a money in your pocket today with a wider distribution network than you can build right away, where you have little control over, or responsibility for, the final product.
- **Indie Publishing** gives you total control and responsibility for every aspect of your book and will cost you a little bit now, with *possible* big rewards later.

Either route comes with a full-time job of marketing your book, if you want to make money at it. Indie Publishing was right for me, but that doesn't mean that Traditional Publishing is wrong for you.

If you are still undecided, do a little research online. Dean Wesley Smith (http://www.deanwesleysmith.com) writes a wonderful blog about Indie Publishing. He's been in the industry a long time and he has a wealth of knowledge, but bear in mind that **he comes to Indie Publishing with an audience in tow.** He's a NY Times Bestselling Author. It's easy for him to make a ton of money right away Indie Publishing. I didn't have an audience to bring to the table, and chances are, you don't either. That can be a game changer and like any business venture, you want to go into this with your eyes open.

Chapter 2: Getting Started

There are six subsections to Chapter 2:

1. Editing your manuscript
2. Beta readers
3. Selecting your book type
4. Cover art
5. Jacket text
6. Author bio

Let's take a look at them one at a time.

1. Edit your manuscript

$ Let me guess: you've been through your book a zillion times, spell checked it six ways to Sunday and your best friend told you it was perfect, right? You still need to find someone to professionally edit it for you. You wrote the book, therefore, you know what is supposed to be on the page. **Your eyes will see what you meant instead of what you wrote.** It happens to everybody.

Your editor should not be your best friend, unless that BFF is also a professional editor who can tell you the cold, honest, painful truth. Remember what you are doing here. You are asking someone to find all of the mistakes and weaknesses in your baby. Nobody likes to hear these things, including me, but this is how we fix them.

Different types of editors

There are many different types of editors out there. You need to know what you are looking for.

- **Content Editor** – A content editor is a full service editor and as such, it is the most expensive of the editors. This person is going to read your manuscript looking for plot holes, character problems, story problems, continuity problems and other structural issues, in addition to looking for mechanical issues.

- **Copy Editors/Line Editors** – A copy editor (often called a line editor) is going to read your manuscript looking for mechanical issues like grammar, punctuation and sentence structure problems, word choice issues (using the right *peak, peek*, or *pique*), and perhaps some continuity problems like "Your hero had blue eyes in the beginning of the story and green eyes at the end," or "You changed the spelling of your heroine's name partway through."
- **Proof Reader** – A proof reader is going to read your manuscript looking for typos, misspellings, some word choice errors and things like that.

Of course, the cost for hiring these people ranges from outrageous to cheap; it all depends on what you are looking for. Content editors are the most expensive and can easily charge between $500 -$1000 depending on the scale of the project. Copy editors generally charge (with lots of swing on both sides of the figure) $1.50 per page that they are going to read. Many prefer to charge a flat rate. A proofreader is going to be the least expensive editor and may be willing to do the work for a couple hundred bucks.

Where can you find an editor?

- Contact the English Literature department of a local college and ask the department head to recommend a student with a keen eye for this sort of thing. Students often work to gain experience and have things to put on their resume. And they are usually cheap.
- Who do you know who likes to read and has a good vocabulary? You might be able to pay a friend in "kind" instead of cash. I have an author friend who is a masseuse and she pays her editor in massages instead of money.

- Contact a local writers' group and see if any members would be interested in editing your book for a nominal fee. RWA, or Romance Writers of America, has chapters all across the country. It's quite possible that you can find an editor there.
- If you want to check out someone specific, my friend and favorite editor, Jane Haertel, often takes on new jobs. You can find information about her services at www.crazydiamondediting.wordpress.com.
- Librarians, secretaries, or teachers are people who probably have the skill to do the job, too.
- If worse comes to worst, you can always Google and find editors galore, but they are likely to cost more.

J's Editor of Choice

Now it just so happens that I majored in English Literature with a concentration in Creative Writing when I was in college. I am confident in my understanding of story structure and my skills with the English language. I'm not saying you need such an education to be a good writer, not at all, but you *do* need to honestly recognize your skills to identify the type of editor you need.

When Jane isn't available, I look for an editor who is somewhere between a proofreader and a copy editor. Homonyms, words like *peak*, *peek* and *pique*, throw me, even though I recognize them when I'm reading. The fact is, I'm a terrible speller and that trips me up. Yes, my spelling skills are so bad, that spell check often doesn't know what word I mean. If the word you typed is spelled correctly (even if it's the wrong *peek*) spell check won't help you out. Grammar check might, but it's wrong often enough that I don't trust it. I know my there/their/they're and my its/it's. Shocking how often grammar check wants me to pick the wrong one!

I learned this the hard way when I didn't hire an editor for my first book and all of the people who read it kindly informed me of every mistake they found. I've got the *peaks* down now, but in my second book I learned that *grill* is a thing you do when cooking and *grille* is the front of a car.

Embarrassing! Thankfully, Jane's the one who caught the grills. I want to turn out the best product I can, the most professional product. I see mistakes in books all the time (especially nowadays when I'm looking for them,) both in Indie Published books and Traditional. But Indie gets a bad rap in this area (not wrap!).

That and Just

The other thing you can do when editing your book is identify those words you over use. We all have 'em. I like the word "just." I don't know why; I just do. "Just" is one of those kind of useless filler words, but I seem to use it to mean: "right now", "barely", "near", "only" and "almost." When I finished my second book, *The Peacock Tale,* I used the **Find** tool in my word processing program and was appalled to see that I had used the word "just" more than 350 times. In a 270 page book. YIKES!

Using **Find and Replace**, I reread each sentence with the word "just" in it and decided if I really needed it there or if another word might be more specific. In the end, I got down to something like ninety-five "justs."

"That" is another one of these often unnecessary words. When I had *The Peacock Tale* edited, I asked the editor to remove "that." She pulled a ton of them out of the story. Identifying these kinds of personal problem areas makes it easy fix them. I still write my first draft the way I think, using "just" and "that." But now, I know to clean them up before it goes to the editor.

The important take-away here is: If you want your book to be a professional product, you must treat it like one and have it edited. Even if you wrote it for your family and nobody else, you should still have another pair of eyes look it over.

And don't forget, if you disagree with some of your editor's recommended changes, you are not obligated to make them. *You* are the author of the book.

2. Beta Readers

Before you publish your book, I recommend that you find a few beta readers. These are folks to give it a read and tell you what they think. I wouldn't have more than three, but I would recommend at least two. Find people you know who like to read in the genre of your book. Their input can be very helpful in identifying holes in the story, or other issues that you haven't seen in the four hundred thirty-seven times you've read the book.

For my second novel, *The Peacock Tale*, I asked two writer friends of mine to read it. The both gave me similar feedback and one of them took the time to somewhat edit the manuscript for me, from a story perspective. Overall, she concluded that the book "just didn't work" for her, which was heartbreaking for me. How could she hate my baby?!

But after a couple of weeks spent digesting the feedback, I had to agree that she was right. I made some significant changes to the story and kept some things where our opinions differed, but in the end, her feedback, however painful to receive, made it a better book.

3. Selecting your book type: print and/or digital

Nowadays, we have two kinds of books to choose from when we publish: print books and digital books, also known as e-books. Some of my books are available in both formats, some are only available in one or the other. It depends on the type of book it is and where the audience is most likely to look for or want it.

Table 2.1 on pages 15 and 16 details which of my books are available in what format and why.

One reason my picture books are available in both print and digital format, even though I sell them almost exclusively as print books, is a marketing purpose. Digital books cost nothing to give away compared to print books which I have to buy. Of course, there may be some lost revenue when giving away digital books, but I consider this an inexpensive bit of marketing. For example, when I get a gig as a guest speaker at a school, if the teachers are using digital technology in the classroom, I might give them a code for a free Dixie & Taco book as a "Thank You" for having me. It doesn't cost me anything, and my book may get in front of new prospective buyers whom I might not have otherwise reached.

The important take-away here is: How you want to sell your books is paramount when thinking about what format to publish them in.

Table 2.1 Why I chose the format I selected

Title	Format	Why
The Cordovan Vault	Print/Digital	These are books 1 and 2 in *The Livingston-Wexford Adventures ("LWA")*, a paranormal adventure series for 'tweens. The audience is mainly 9-14
The Peacock Tale	Print/Digital	year old kids and that market segment is reading more print today than they are digital. It may change and bears watching. It doesn't cost anything to make the books available digitally, and therefore I have, but I'm focused on selling print copies of these titles.
The Fearsome Dane	Primarily Digital	This is a side story to *LWA*. It's a tragic romance novella and is intended for a slightly more mature audience. It'll primarily be available as an e-book, priced at $.99 but I will have print copies in case someone wanted the complete *LWA* collection.
Gastric-Genealogy	Print/ CD-Rom	This is a cookbook/family tree. The audience for this is really just my family or folks who might be attracted to the recipes. *Gastric-Genealogy* will only be available in print; however the template will be available on CD-Rom for folks who might like to write a version for their family.

(Table 2.1 continued)

Title	Format	Why
The Adventures of Dixie & Taco	Primarily Print	Dixie & Taco's kindergarten series is a collection of books written for emerging readers. Common kindergarten sight words are in blue text as a visual cue for the parents to let the kids try to read those words. Primarily, these are sold as print books so that they can be "personalized" for a town's kindergarten reading curriculum, but since it's free to make them digital, they are available that way, too.
Brook the Fish	Primarily Print	Brook the Fish is a beginning reader for first graders. Primarily these are sold as print books, but it is available digitally as well.

4. Cover Art

We all judge books by their cover. I'm sorry if this comes as a shock to you, but you do it, too. What makes you pick up an unknown book in a store and consider buying it? Either the author's name or, in most other cases, the cover art. You need to create eye-catching cover art for your book no matter how you decide to publish it.

Creating Cover Art for Print Books

- Createspace.com (a POD company that produces print books – see page 25 for a definition) has plenty of free cover art template options to choose from, each with its own set of variable details such as text color, background color, font, etc.
- You can create your own cover in MS PowerPoint or a similar program and upload it to Createspace.

- Be sure that you have the legal right to use any images you add to the picture.
- There are many websites where you can buy $ pictures. I use iStockphoto.com. You will want to read the terms and conditions carefully, but my understanding of the agreement is that you can use their images up to 500,000 times, collectively. If you substantially modify the image, then the rules loosen up. I'm not a lawyer, so if you have questions of liability you should consult someone who is.
- You can hire someone to create the cover for you. $ If you don't know anyone with the skill to do it, try contacting a local college art department (or high school art department, for that matter) and offer a nominal fee to a student to create it for you.
  - I have also had wonderful luck with a free online service called iFreelance.com. You can post a job there (for free) and artists looking for work will bid on your project. You pay the artist directly.
  - If you hire someone to create cover art for you, be clear with the person you hire about who will retain the copyright to the art. If you agree that it's a "Work for Hire" project then you, the book author/ employer, will retain the copyright to the art and you can do what you want with it.

Creating Cover Art for E-Books

Creating a cover for an e-book is even easier.

- Create your cover in a program like MS PowerPoint and save it as a .jpg file. Use Save as and drop down the file types.
- Be sure you have the legal right to use any images you add to the picture.

5. Jacket Text

Once you've created intriguing cover art, you need to follow that up with Buy-Me text on the back of the book or in the description field for an e-book. The cover is going to attract people browsing for books. The jacket text is where you convert browsers into buyers. Consider these ideas when writing your jacket text:

<u>For Fiction Books:</u>

- Who are the characters?
- What is the conflict?
- What audience is this book appropriate for?
- Leave the reader guessing so that they want to buy the book.

Let's take a look at the jacket text for my book *The Cordovan Vault*:

> Kayla and Quinn are having a *really* bad weekend. For 14-year old enemies whose normal life means that they are forced to live together because her brother married his sister, it takes something extraordinary for things to be *really* bad.
>
> Like their house exploding.
> Or people trying to kill them.
>
> When a mysterious DVD turns up with the message "We are not who you think we are," they begin a crazy adventure to figure out what that means and they find that nothing is the way it seems.

Who are the characters? Kayla and Quinn. We know there are male and female protagonists.

What is the conflict? These kids are enemies, but are stuck together. Things are bad. Their house explodes, people are trying to kill them. Conflict galore.

18

What audience is the book for? The characters are kids and there is a mystery afoot. Their age implies that the book would be for kids a few years younger since kids like to read up (read about characters who are a few years older than they are.)

Leave the reader guessing. "We are not who you think we are." Well then, who are they? If nothing is the way it seems, what is different and how?

For Non-Fiction:

- Hook the reader into taking more than a passing glance at your text.
- What is the topic?
- What secrets are you going to impart that the reader can't get elsewhere?
- Why should the reader select your book over that of your competitor?
- Why should the reader trust you?

Now, let's take a look at the text from the back of this book:

Have you dreamed of being a published author? The Indie Publishing phenomenon means you absolutely can make your dream a reality!

Indie Publishing is short for Independent Publishing. It's easy and incredibly affordable. Print books often cost less than $5.00 per copy and at least one vendor has no minimum number of copies required at purchase. You can buy one if you want to! And publishing digital books is free. FREE!

DIY Publishing ~ Cheap & Easy takes you step-by-step through the process necessary to format your existing manuscript and publish it in both print and digital form.

- **Scary Terminology** is defined in language that is easily understood by lay people.
- **Format Your Book** for publication yourself, following the steps outlined in Chapter 3.
- Compare **Publishing Formats** to decide which is right for you.
- Create a **Marketing Mind Map** and brainstorm ideas for how to sell your book.
- Use the **Checklists** that summarize each chapter to be sure you took all the right steps.

J Monkeys is an Indie Published author and this book is an example of an Indie Publication. J had always dreamed of being a published author and, in 2011, that dream came true. *DIY Publishing ~ Cheap & Easy* gives you the opportunity to learn from J's experiences, successes, mistakes and missteps publishing eight books in this new and dynamic aspect of the publishing industry.

If you have a manuscript you want to publish and you're thinking about skipping the whole Agent/Traditional Publishing Firm thing, consider Indie Publishing as a viable alternative. *DIY Publishing ~ Cheap & Easy* explains how to do it.

Hook the reader into taking more than a passing glance at your text. Have you dreamed of being a published author? If you think "Why, yes I have!" then you're hooked and you'll read further.

What is the topic? The next bit identifies the topic of the book and defines Indie Publishing.

What secrets are you going to impart that the reader can't get elsewhere? Indie Publishing is easy and affordable. Then there is a bulleted list of things that might be of particular interest.

Why should the reader select your book over that of your competitor? This book is a step-by-step manual on how to publish your book.

Why should the reader trust you? I'm livin' the dream, man! I am an Indie Published author and this very book you hold in your hand is an example of an Indie Publication.

6. Author Bio

You need to write an author bio. Save it somewhere you can find it easily; you'll use it in lots of places. The author bio should be a paragraph of about five sentences or even two paragraphs totaling six or seven sentences. Readers will want to know a little bit about you, enough to determine if they might like your book. This is also a great opportunity to plug your next project, if you've got one in the hopper.

The author bio should cover:

- Who are you?
- Why do you write or how did you get into it?
- Why did you write this?
- What are you writing next and when will it be available?

I have two slightly different bios, one for my 'Tween Adventure series and one for my Picture Books. Take a look.

Livingston-Wexford Author bio:

> J Monkeys has always been a storyteller, although mostly just for self-entertainment. J was shocked to learn that everybody didn't spend their time with their head in a cloud imagining what they would do if some kind of adventure presented itself. After getting a degree in Creative Writing from the University of Connecticut (Go Huskies!) and spending WAY too long writing boring things

for a regular paycheck, J is proud to be a novelist, at last.

J lives in Connecticut with a menagerie of children and pets and is hard at work on the next book in the Livingston-Wexford series – The Orange Trade. Look for it in 2013.

The first paragraph gives some information about me. I've always had stories in my head and have entertained myself with them as long as I can remember. I studied writing in college and then made a living at it for a while, but not as a fiction writer.

The first paragraph is intended to convey to the reader that I'm just a regular person, I'm quirky and I know how to write. Also, can you tell my gender from that paragraph? Nope, and that's intentional. There is some thought that twelve year old boys don't like to read books written by women. That's why JK Rowling is JK and not Joanne Rowling. Oh dear, I may have just given it all away. Shhhh – don't tell anybody, okay?

Now the second paragraph places me in the USA, in New England and in Connecticut. Where an author lives (in general, not their address) is always interesting to me. It gives them some specificness (yes, I just made up that word. We're writers, we can do that.) that I find lends credibility to the writing. I don't know why. And of course, you see the author's location on biographies all the time.

Now take a look at my Picture Book bio:

J Monkeys has always been a storyteller, although mostly just for self-entertainment. J was shocked to learn that everybody didn't spend their time with their head in a cloud imagining what they would do if some kind of adventure presented itself. After getting a degree in Creative Writing from the University of Connecticut (Go Huskies!) and spending WAY too long writing boring things for a regular paycheck, J is proud to be a published author at long last.

J was inspired to write the Dixie and Taco picture book series by the real-life Dixie. When Dixie was in kindergarten, she was convinced that she couldn't read, even though Dixie knew the sight words her class was learning. The picture books Dixie was reading didn't have enough of her sight words in them, or the font was too small, or the words were all over the page and Dixie had trouble following them. So, being a loving parent, J wrote a book to fix all those problems.

The first paragraph is the same in both bios. But in the second paragraph, I wanted to establish my bona fides when it comes to writing for a beginning reader. I don't have any credentials in teaching reading, other than a kid in my life who is struggling with it. I made a list of all the problems she was having and wrote some books that address those issues. I listed those issues, briefly, in that second paragraph, hoping that other parents would recognize them as problems their own kids have and would want to buy my books.

The important take-away here is: The author bio is mostly written for marketing purposes. Keep that in mind when you are writing yours. Also, don't be afraid to modify it to support your current/next book.

Chapter 3:

Formatting Matters ~ Print Books

If you do not want to have print books and only want to e-publish, you can skip this chapter. But, if you do want print books, do it **BEFORE** you e-publish. Trust me on this. You'll save yourself many, many hours of work.

Great! Your manuscript content has been reviewed by a third party editor and all of your edits are complete. It is as perfect as it's going to be. Now let's make this thing look like a book.

$ Formatting your book for print is one of those jobs that you can pay someone else to do for you, but if you have fairly good skills with your word processing program (not necessarily expert skills), there is no reason why you can't do it yourself and save the money. It will take some time, but not too much.

I use the 2010 version of MS Word, and I print my books through Createspace.com. I'll be referencing those tools when I discuss how to format for print, but other word processing programs use similar features.

Formatting is really quite easy, just a pain in the booty. There is a bit of scary industry terminology that you need to know. Table 3.1 lays it out for you.

Table 3.1: Scary Terminology – part 1

Term	Definition
Print on demand or POD	This is a type of printing company for physical books. Print on demand or POD allows people to buy exactly the number of copies of a book that they want. You are not required to buy hundreds of copies; you can buy as few as one copy. However, bookstores rarely buy POD because they can't return them if they don't sell.
Trim Size	This is the name for the size of your book after it's been bound and trimmed. There are many industry standard sizes to choose from.
Front Matter	Front matter is all the stuff that comes before the first page of the text. This is a place to record your copyright, the ISBN (see below,) disclaimer, cover artist, date and location of publication, your dedication or acknowledgements, a table of contents or any other information.
ISBN	ISBN is an acronym for International Standard Book Number. The ISBN is a unique identifier that allows a seller to find a specific book produced by a specific publisher. ISBNs come in 10 and 13 digit lengths.

There are seven sections to this chapter:

1. The Big Backward P
2. Size Matters
3. Mirror Margins
4. Take a Break
5. Headers & Footers
6. Copyright Notice & Other Front Matter
7. PDF-ing

Let's take a look at them one at a time.

1. The Big Backward P

The very first thing you want to do is **turn on your show/hide**, otherwise known as The Big Backward P. This is a VERY useful tool, if you aren't already familiar with it. It allows you to see spaces between words (represented as a dot) and spaces between lines, section breaks and page breaks (big difference! Don't worry, we'll get to it,) headers and footers, and all sorts of stuff. If you want your layout to be perfect, you need to be able to see these things to fix them. Turn on show/hide. In MS Word 2010, you just click the ¶ button. Well, it kinda looks like that. It's right up there, at the top of the Home tab, just a hitch to the right of center. Did you find it? Excellent!

2. Size Matters!

Next - what size do you want your print book to be?

Table 3.2: Industry Standard Sizes and Genres

Size (in inches)	Common Uses
4 x 6.75	Mass market paperbacks (printed in big bulk quantities and sized to minimize production waste)
5.25 x 8	Young Adult fiction
5.5 x 8.25	Novels, Trade paperbacks
5.5 x 8.5	Comic books, Comic book digests
6 x 9	Handbooks, Trade paperbacks, Children's picture books
7 x 10	Textbooks
7.5 x 9.25	Gift books, Art books, Manuals
8 x 10	Children's picture books
8.5 x 11	Manuals, Textbooks, Magazines, Souvenir books

Once you decide what size book to make, you need to prepare your manuscript accordingly. Documents in a word processing program default to the size paper your printer is likely to spit out. In the United States, that's 8.5 x 11 paper. Other parts of the world use A4 paper. You need to make your document size match the size you intend to print.

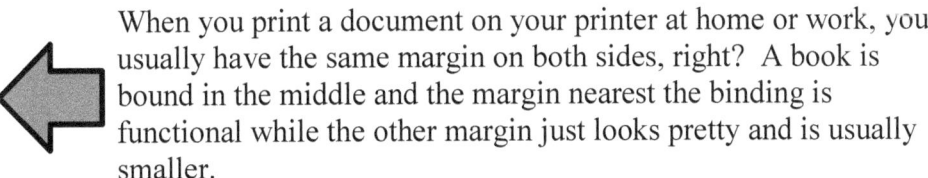 **To change the size of your document**, go into the Page Layout area of your document, choose Size, Custom Sizes or More Paper Sizes, and change the Height and Width to match your intended size. If you have section breaks in your document (as this one does) you might need to highlight the entire document, then modify the size, or select "whole document" from the drop down box at the bottom of the page layout screen.

Now that you've modified your paper size, you need to go look at your paragraphs again. With smaller paper, your paragraphs may now be grammatically correct, but visually too long. As a reader, you know that paragraphs which go on forever do so unread. We skip down to the next bit of action or dialogue. Use your own judgment, but paragraphs that are much longer than two inches are visually too long.

I've found that it's easier for me to decide on a book size before I begin writing it, that way I set my document up when I start writing and it's less work later on. Yes, I learned this the hard way.

3. Mirror Your Margins

When you print a document on your printer at home or work, you usually have the same margin on both sides, right? A book is bound in the middle and the margin nearest the binding is functional while the other margin just looks pretty and is usually smaller.

To mirror margins, go to Page Layout, Margins, Custom Margin, on the drop down next to Pages (½ way down the Custom Page – Margin's tab) click the arrow and select Mirror Margins.

Click the View menu. Click the icon for Two Pages. This lets you see what your open book will look like. Sorta.

Your word processor defaults to the idea that your first page is a left hand page, but a book opens with a right facing page. Are you with me? I think this is the most confusing thing about the whole Indie Publishing DIY formatting thing: your screen is showing you the opposite of what you will see in print form. I'm going to write that again, and bold it because it's that important.

Your computer screen is showing the pages of your soon-to-be paper book on the opposite side of how it will look when you print it. Let me show you. Here's a picture of the first two pages of this book on my computer:

DIY PUBLISHING

CHEAP & EASY

A step-by-step guide to

Independent Publishing

for authors

by

J Monkeys

Flip to the front of this book and compare. See that the DIY Pub page is actually on the right side of the open book, not the left as shown on the screen, and you don't see the copyright page until you turn the title page over. This is what I'm writing about here.

It's okay. There's no need to freak out – just be aware of this fundamental difference between the two mediums. When I'm putting the finishing touches on a draft before ordering a proof copy, I sometimes add a blank page (with a section break see p. 30) to the very beginning of the manuscript so I can see my manuscript the way it will print.

Like this:

<table>
<tr>
<td>

Section break
</td>
<td>

DIY Publishing
Cheap & Easy
A step-by-step guide to
Independent Publishing
for authors

by
J Monkeys
</td>
</tr>
</table>

This is especially helpful when I'm editing a picture book and I want to see if the text on the left page lines up with the text on the right page. And I like to be sure the pages facing each other look good together. After I had the final art from the illustrator for *Dixie and Taco go to the Zoo,* looking at the book this way gave me the idea to re-order some of the pages/pictures. I think it made the story better.

Without that blank page in the computer version, you should be aware that the location of your page number (you've added pages numbers, right? No? We'll get there in a few pages.) will be in the opposite place. Page numbers are usually on the outside corner of the page, but on your computer they will be on the inside corner, where the binding will be on the book.

Don't forget to delete that extra blank beginning page before you PDF. (See section 7, p. 42.)

4. Take a break. Page break or section break, that is.

Page breaks/section breaks are another one of those annoyingly tricky little things. Thankfully, your active show/hide will tell you which one you have. But what are they anyway?

Page breaks: a page break moves your text to the next page. **Section breaks:** a section break gives you advanced formatting capability for that section of your document. It will also move your text to the next page, if you choose that option.

You are going to need to do some advanced formatting here. Don't worry, it's not difficult. If I can do it, so can you.

⊠ When I'm working with my print book document, I don't use page breaks. I use section breaks. Section breaks mean that I can move my page numbers to where I really want them and modify the header on the page as well. I recommend that you go back through your document and change all of your page breaks to Section breaks / Next page.

To do that in MS Word 2010, you click the Page Layout tab, then about a third of the way across the options, choose the drop down arrow next to Breaks. Now you have some choices. The top half are Page Break options. Ignore those for now. The second half are Section Break options.

- **Section break / Next page** – this is the option I use instead of Page Break. It moves all of the subsequent text down to the next page.
- **Section break / Continuous** – I use this option to create a new section when I don't want to move text. I might do this to modify a header/footer or do some other bit of formatting.
- **Section break / Even page** – Honestly, I have no idea what this one is for. I've never used it.

- **Section break / Odd page** – I've never used this one either.

Yes, doing this is a pain in the backside because you have to do it for each section/chapter. But if you don't do it, you'll be frustrated to baldness by your inability to make your formatting look the way you want. I'm telling you, save yourself the headache and just change these now. It will only take a few minutes. Well, maybe thirty minutes, depending on the length of your document.

5. Headers and Footers

For the uninitiated, your word processing program will allow you to put text in the top (head) and bottom (foot) margins of your document. Hence, headers and footers.

I will tell you the truth here – I've spent more time fighting with headers and footers on my manuscript than probably all the other parts of the formatting combined. I just haven't found an easy way to do it, yet. I'm sure there is one...if one of you finds it, please contact me and tell me what it is. I'm serious. My email address is: jmonkey.writer@gmail.com.

But until an easier way to do this presents itself, here's the path I've slogged along.

First, imagine, or scribble on a piece of paper, what you want the top margin and bottom margin of your book to look like. Flip through a bunch of your favorite books and see how they did it. I recommend something simple just to limit your frustrations, but you can put any kind of text/symbols in the header/footer margin you want.

It's common for fiction books to have the author's name in the header on the left pages and the title of the book or chapter in the header on the right pages. But there's a lot of flexibility in this. I just glanced at a few books on my shelf and they were all over the place.

- A bunch of romance novels, by various authors and publishers, hard cover and paperback, all had the author's name on the left and the title of the book on the right.
- The *Harry Potter* books by JK Rowling (at least the American version) has the chapter number on the left pages and the chapter title on the right.
- *Twilight* by Stephenie Meyer has no header at all, but the page number in the center of the footer has an artistic little flourish on either side of it.
- *Artemis Fowl* by Eoin Colfer has the page numbers in the header and some kind of runic scrawl in the footer.
- *Eragon* by Christopher Paolini has no header or footer, and the page numbers in the outer left/right margin.
- *The Nosferatu Scroll* by James Becker has both the page number and the author name/book title in the header and there is nothing in the footer. Diana Gabaldon's *The Fiery Cross* has the same setup.

The good news is there are lots of options. Decide what you want and then plug it in.

Now a word about Headers and Footers before I tell you how to do it – I think this is the hardest of the lot. Don't get frustrated. Pull your manuscript file up and try some of these things rather than just reading through this section. Even I got overwhelmed when I was reading through it...and I wrote it!

To add the header in MS Word 2010, go to Insert, and click the drop down arrow below Header and choose Edit Header. This will bring you to the Header/Footer view. If your page is now blank, check the "Show Document Text" box at the top and your text will show in gray.

You can type your header into the space provided. Format it as you wish, centered or not, all caps, small caps, or in a funky font. It will now be in the header on every page unless you tell your word processor differently. This is where section breaks come in to play.

If you decide to have one header on the left and a different header on the right, like the romance novels I mentioned above, check off the "Different Odd & Even Pages" box.

Do you want your header to start on the first page of the document? Probably not. There's a box to check, "Different First Page". But you probably don't want your header in the front matter. And you may not want it on the opening pages of your chapters, either. Designate those pages as a Different First Page.

⊠ Open up your header view again. In MS Word 2010, go to Insert, and click the drop down arrow below Header and choose Edit Header. Do you see the small box just under the header boundary? It says, Odd (or Even) page, Section 4 (or some other number) and on the right under that same boundary, reads the oh-so-important phrase "Same as previous."

The headers and footers in your document are all linked to the previous section. If you want your sections to be different, you have to **break those links**! You can't do this with page breaks. That's why I use section breaks in the print book formatting.

You may find that you need to add a Section Break/Continuous somewhere on the first page of each chapter. I do this to ensure that the first page of the chapter doesn't have a heading. It creates a short section with no header, but allows the rest of the chapter to have the header by breaking that "Same as Previous" link.

Now, let the real fight begin. I'm going to add a header to this document right now. I'll add the book title to the left hand pages and the chapter title to the right and carry it forward throughout the rest of the book, without modifying the header-less earlier chapters. Here I go – wish me luck.

For the even pages:

- I scrolled to the beginning of this chapter and clicked at the top of the page to tell MS Word where I wanted to begin my header.
- I clicked Insert, the Header drop down arrow, Edit Header.
- I unchecked the "Different First Page" box and it changed from a "First Page" to an "Even Page."
- I clicked in the Header area and typed the title of the book. Yes, I decided on the title right now. I Googled the title I wanted and checked Amazon – neither returned a book by this exact title, so I'm going with it!
- I clicked Home and played around with fonts (click the Font drop down arrow for options) until I found Poor Richard. I decided that it was fun but professional and a bit artistic and would look good on the cover of the book. I selected font size 14, went with small caps and centered it.
- I clicked the "Link to Previous" button (just above "Navigation".) The "Same as Previous" tag on the right side blinked off.

For the odd pages:

- I scrolled down to the next page, still in the Header view. I typed in the Header "Chapter 3: Formatting Matters – Print Books."
- I modified the font to match the previous Header style.
- I unchecked the "Different First Page" box.
- I clicked the "Link to Previous" button to break the link.

Hey, guess what? It didn't work properly! Sigh. ☹ I went back into the header view to see what was going on, and for some reason, MS Word chose to add my header to page four of the document. I removed it and broke several other links to previous pages.

Now I can scroll through my active document (you can get out of the header view by double clicking on the document text. You can get into the header view the same way. Double click on the header.) and see that the opening pages, including the Table of Contents and Chapters One and Two have no header. Yippeeee!

☹ Unfortunately, I've noticed that the first line of this page is too close to the header, in my opinion. Don't you agree?

To modify this, I went to Page Layout, Margins, Custom Margin, Layout tab, Margin tab and looked to see how the Header and Top Margin were set up. It turned out that they were both set to 0.5". I modified the Top Margin to be 1.0" to add more space.

Making this change would normally mean that I have to go back through the document to be sure that everything still lines up the way I want it. I suspect that some of the tables or Section Break – Next Pages might get messed up. But, because I wanted you, dear author, to see what I was talking about, I'm going to modify the spacing between the first line of the page and the header beginning with the next section by doing it on the next page and choosing the "This point forward" option in the drop down at the bottom of the Margin tab.

Footers

Let's look at **footers** for a minute. Basically the process is the same, except that you are modifying footers instead of headers. You will still have to break links when things aren't lining up the way you want them.

To add page numbers in MS Word 2010, click Insert, then the Page Number drop down. This gives you options to put your page number at the top of the page, the bottom or the side. You can also edit your page numbers (by clicking Format Page Number, highlight the number, right click and make your selection) to either continue numbering from the previous section, or modify the starting number, or both.

Oh, yes. Doesn't this look much better than on the previous page? This line isn't all smooshed up against the header. To apply the change going forward: in the Margin box, at the bottom, I clicked the drop down next to "Apply to:" and changed it from "This Section" to "This Point Forward." It was wonky when I did it the first time, it changed page 35, too. So I added a Section Break/Continuous at the end of the previous page – just after "both." You can't tell, but trust me, it's there. And now my header is right where I want it.

You may notice that page one of this book is actually the fifth page of the document. I started numbering the pages in that section, changed the beginning number from 5 to 1 in the Page Number Format box. Then, I had the rest of the sections of the document be the "Same as Previous." Diabolical, I know.

The important take-away here is: headers and footers are really the bane of my publishing existence, but it's doable. Don't get too frustrated. I honestly spent several hours fussing with the headers and footers in my first novel, *The Cordovan Vault,* while using an older version of MS Word. Then when I was wrapping up the draft of *The Peacock Tale*, I had the newer version and I had to spend hours figuring it all out again. Frustrating!

If you find that you need help with this formatting stuff, find a friend who is a secretary or high school/college student. Those people know the ins and outs of word processing programs and would likely be happy to help. My husband is a Tech Guy (as opposed to a Car Guy or Sports Guy) and he couldn't help me with formatting. He can rebuild my computer from a paper clip and spare wire (ala MacGyver!) but his skillset doesn't require him to know this deep level formatting stuff.

And I'm happy to say, headers and footers are the hardest of the lot. If you live through that, you can do it all!

6. Front Matter and Copyright Notice

There are a few other (simpler!) things to consider before you PDF your document and send it off for printing.

You need to create your front matter. Front matter is all the stuff that comes before the first page of the text. This is a place to record your copyright notice, the ISBN, disclaimer, cover artist, your dedication or acknowledgements, a table of contents or any other information.

You need a title page as the first page of your book. The title page usually has the book title, the author's name and any other major contributors.

The flip side of the title page is the place to record a number of things, including your copyright notice, the typical legalese statement of "Dude, don't sue me!" and your ISBN numbers (you can get them free from Createspace for your print book.)

Copyright Law

Right off the bat here, let me tell you that I am NOT a lawyer. Any questions you have related to the legalities of copyright law should be individually addressed by someone trained to answer them. What I can tell you, is my *understanding* of the law and how I apply that understanding in my own "original works of authorship." Plagiarism (or the act of stealing someone else's work and passing it off as your own either for monetary gain or not) is illegal. It's stealing. It's not okay in any circumstances. Don't do it.

What is copyright?

You can find the 1976 Copyright Act and all of its amendments online. Check www.copyright.gov.

The Copyright Office has a great flier, called Circular 1, that reviews US Copyright Law. I'm going to paraphrase a few of the highlights from that Circular here, but if you are interested in this stuff, you might want to read the original. You can find it at: http://www.copyright.gov/circs/circ1.pdf.

Copyright is legal protection from plagiarism. Copyright protection exists from the time your work is "created in fixed form." That's a fancy legal way of saying "written down," basically. Copyright doesn't protect an idea, but once you take that idea and flesh it out into a "work" you're covered.

Copyright notice is that blurb on the inside of the title page on pretty much any book on your shelf. Copyright notice is no longer required by copyright law, however it can be beneficial. The notice identifies the copyright owner and the year of first publication. You can't go wrong with a copyright notice, and it's free, so it's a good idea to include it.

The proper form for copyright notice is:

- The word Copyright and the copyright symbol (©).
- The year of first publication.
- The name of the copyright owner.

For example: the copyright notice on this book is:

Copyright © 2014 Jennifer Moncuse

 To add the copyright symbol in MS Word 2010, click Insert, then click Symbol (all the way to the right), more symbols (if it's not right there), select the symbol from the normal text and click insert. You can also press alt + ctrl + C at the same time on your keyboard.

A note about pseudonyms: US Copyright law grants 70 years of protection after an author dies when the author's name is on the copyright notice. It grants 95 years of protection from the copyright date for works published under a pseudonym "when the author's identity is not revealed in the records of the Copyright Office" according to US Copyright Circular 1 page 4/5.

The statement "All rights reserved. Except as permitted under the U.S. Copyright Act of 1976, no part of this publication may be reproduced, distributed or transmitted in any form or by any means, or stored in a database or retrieval system, without the prior written permission of the author" is also part of the copyright notice that was required prior to January 1, 1978. This is no longer required for copyright protection, but is still common.

Copyright registration is a voluntary legal formality, but there are some benefits that may make it worth the nominal fee.

- While an unregistered work is protected under the law, you can't sue for infringement unless you register.
- If you are registered before the infringement occurs (as opposed to after the infringement but before you sue,) there are additional damages and things that you could be entitled to.
- Registration also meets the mandatory deposit requirement because you have to send a copy of the book with your registration.

Registration can be done online or via a paper form. Either way, go to www.copyright.gov to find further information on registration.

Copyright law does require a publisher to make a **Mandatory Deposit** of two copies of all books published in the United States to the Library of Congress. If you are the publisher, then you have to comply with the requirement. The address is:

> Library of Congress
> Copyright Office CAD 407
> 101 Independence Ave SE
> Washington, DC 20559-6607

What if I e-publish and don't make a physical book?

This is a fabulous question! The current US Copyright Law was written in 1976, long before there were e-books. There is an exemption to the mandatory deposit requirement if your book is only available online but there is also a statement that if your book is available in a "machine readable format," like on a computer, then there *is* a deposit requirement. This seems to be a gray area, although a February 24, 2010 interim regulation strongly implies that e-book don't fall into the machine readable format category. Perhaps the rise in e-publication is too new to have given life to clear cut laws. If you have specific questions on this matter, you may want to consult an attorney.

The "Dude, don't sue me" statement

Go pull any piece of fiction off your shelf and flip to the inside of the title page. You will see a statement that says something like "This book is a work of fiction. Names, characters, places and incidents are the product of the author's imagination or are used fictitiously. Any resemblance to actual events, locales or persons living or dead, is coincidental." Go ahead, look.

Did you find it? I like to call this the "Dude, don't sue me" statement. In our litigious society, you could be sued if someone thinks that you based a character on them and it reflects badly on them. If you say it, it could be slander. If you write it down, it could be libel. It's a good idea, and common practice, to include a "Dude, don't sue me" statement in the book and you may want to do so.

If you decide to include the exact "Dude don't sue me" statement that I added two paragraphs back, it's not plagiarism. It's common practice that all fiction has that statement. I even saw it as part of the rolling credits at the end of a movie last night. As the movie was *Snow White and the Huntsman*, I'm pretty sure nobody is going to say that the movie was based on him. Or her. It's just common practice.

ISBN

The International Standard Book Number, or ISBN, is a worldwide, unique book identifier. You need to have one for people to find and buy your book.

(My editor extraordinaire put a note here in my manuscript that has a good point. She's never found or bought a book by searching for its ISBN and come to think of it, neither have I. So why do you need an ISBN? You need an ISBN to get a LCCN or Library of Congress Control Number. If you plan to pitch your book to libraries, they may require an LCCN. The day may come when you don't need an ISBN, but for now, it's common practice and you can get them for free, so why not include it? Plus it adds to your "real book" factor.)

The ISBN identifies one edition of a book from one publisher. If you plan to have multiple editions of your book (a print edition and an e-book edition, for example) you will need to have multiple ISBNs.

ISBNs are sold to "publishers." If you would like to purchase your own ISBN from a licensed ISBN broker you can do that and you will be listed as the publisher of record for your book. I've seen ISBNs from licensed brokers priced like this: 1 ISBN for $125, 10 ISBNs for $250, 100 ISBNs for $575 and up. Most books require more than one ISBN. One licensed ISBN broker is Bowker. You can find more information at their website: http://www.bowker.com/en-US/products/servident_isbn.shtml.

Now, I'm a small business owner. I'm very selective about how I spend my *very* limited business budget. Having my own ISBN is not something that's important to me. That's why I choose to use the free ISBN given to me by Createspace. Doing so does make Createspace the publisher of record, but it doesn't give them any rights to my work. Flip to page 47 and I'll walk you through the process of setting up your Createspace ISBN.

I've also printed books with Lulu, another print on demand company and I was able to get a free ISBN from them as well. You can learn more about Lulu at www.lulu.com.

Other Front Matter

Are there any **other contributors** to your book that you'd like to mention? Did someone create illustrations or cover art for you? The title page is a nice place to mention that. Typically, editors are not mentioned as contributors.

Are your **dedicating** your book to anyone? Are there others you'd like to acknowledge? Did someone offer their expertise? While editors aren't usually contributors, they are frequently seen in the **acknowledgements**. Dedications and acknowledgements are the same thing. Usually, you'd have one or the other.

Do you have a **Table of Contents** or a chapter list? That's front matter, too. Most mainstream fiction does not have a TOC, but Middle Grade/YA fiction often does. Non-fiction usually does.

Do you have a list of other books you have published? Add that in also.

All right! You are almost done! Your edits are complete. Your formatting is complete. Your front matter is complete. Exciting times! There's just one more thing to consider before you PDF that document. (See section 7 below.)

What are you putting at the end of the book? Presumably, your audience will finish reading your book and think to himself/herself, "Wow. That was great! Where can I find more?" You might consider adding your author biography to the end of your document. If you have another work that you will be publishing soon (like in the next six months) add an excerpt. Do you have a website? Add the web address with a line like, "Find out more about author J Monkeys at www.jmonkeys.com."

7. PDF-ing

The computer software company, Adobe, created the Portable Document Format way back in the Internet's infancy and now it's the industry standard. A PDF is a graphic file of your document. Imagine that some fancy computer camera looked at your document and took a picture of it, exactly the way you created it. That's a PDF. You will upload the PDF version to your POD company for them to print.

Once you have a complete document with everything you need for a complete book, PDF the document. Createspace has a new process where they'll PDF it for you if you upload an MS Word document. Other POD companies may not offer this service for free. PDFing isn't difficult and it's a good way to protect your work. Other people can't make changes to PDFs as easily as they can to an MS Word document. And doing it yourself gives you a chance to ensure that it converts correctly before your upload.

To create a PDF in MS Word 2010, all you have to do is select PDF from the drop down list of file types when you use the File/Save As function. It's very easy and PDFs my documents perfectly every time.

When I published my first book, I was using a free word processing program that didn't have PDFing capability. I downloaded several different PDF tools and none of them gave me the ability to create a PDF document in a size other than 8.5 x 11. This was a HUGE problem. Even though I had modified the paper size in the original document, that sizing didn't carry over to the PDF. I spent hours trying to fix this and finally resorted to emailing the document to a friend who PDF'd it for me.

That wasn't an ideal situation, however. Every time you make a change to your document (and believe me, you aren't done making changes yet) you will have to wait to have your friend PDF it again.

Then I found that for a very small fee (it varied between $0.25 and $2.00 depending on who was charging me) the office supply store Staples could make a PDF for me and save it to my flash drive. This was better, but I still found myself making late night trips to Staples for PDFing.

In the end, changing to a better word processing program gave me PDF capability whenever I wanted it.

Save your document as a PDF and you are ready to upload to your on-demand printer.

Chapter 4:
Upload Your Book For Print

⊠ All PDF'd and ready to go? Sweet! Did you double check to be sure that your PDF document is the right size? Hover your mouse over the bottom left corner of the PDF document for a few seconds and the size will pop up.

If you plan to have your book available in both print and digital format, I'm here to tell you from experience, **review your proof copy before you create the digital edition**. You might want to review two or even three proofs before you are ready to say that your print book is finalized and ready for the public.

A **proof copy** is really just one printed book, but the last page has the word "proof" slanted across the blank space. This means it's a draft copy. You absolutely will find things to change in your proof copy when you read it. Maybe it will be something small, like a misplaced header, or you might not like the way something looks. You may find lots of little things. My first proof usually ends up full of scratch-outs and changes. That's the point of having a proof copy.

When you create the digital edition of your book for an e-reader, it has to be formatted again. This means you will have at least two versions of your book and every time you make a change to the text in one, you need to make that change in the other, too. The first thing you do when formatting your digital edition is remove the page numbers. E-readers allow the reader to modify the font size to whatever is comfortable for them. Where the page breaks is different from reader to reader depending on how they have their device set up. Page numbers are obsolete in a digital edition.

Without page numbers, making updates to match your digital and print versions is very time consuming. That's why I will never make that mistake again! **Finalize your print version**. Order as many proofs as you need to be confident that your work is ready for release. **THEN** make your digital edition.

Where do I get a proof copy?

I print most of my books with Createspace. There absolutely are other POD (Print on Demand) companies out there. Lulu and Lightening Source are two examples. But, I LOVE Createspace so I'm going to walk you through setup and ordering your proof copy with that company. Other POD companies have similar setup steps.

One consideration when choosing your POD company is this: Createspace currently has a 24-page minimum size. One of my picture books is shorter than that. I used Lulu to print it and I'm very happy with the quality of their work, but Lulu's pricing was more expensive than Createspace. (See the side note below for more detail.) But the set up process was largely the same on both websites.

A printing side note: I printed *Brook the Fish* with a different sort of printing company, PrintPlace.com. They typically make brochures and other marketing collateral. I decided to give them a try because I wasn't happy with the price of that book with Lulu. These would be copies for me to take to a school and sign/sell there. Lulu's price for this book, to me is $9.30, to the general public it's $12.00. As a parent, $12 for a paperback picture book is a bit steep. And as an author, I'm only getting $2.70 per book. Plus, I doubt I'll sell very many at that high price point.

PrintPlace.com's pricing is very competitive but you have to order in high volume. I ordered 500 copies of the book for $616 including shipping. That's $1.25 per copy compared with $9.30 per copy from Lulu. That means I can sell *Brook the Fish* at $6.00 a copy and make $4.75 per book. For me, that's a much better price point and profit margin.

Createspace.com is part of the Amazon family and these days, when I think books, I think Amazon. My experiences with Createspace's customer service department have been nothing short of top notch and the books look great. And of course, the most important question for someone doing this on the cheap – the books are totally affordable! All of the books I've published so far (including this one) have cost me about $5.00 per copy (except for *Brook the Fish*. See the side note on page 46 for detail.) That means I can sell them for an affordable price and hopefully (someday) make some money for my trouble.

Setting up a book for printing with Createspace is really quite easy. There is only a little bit of scary terminology for you to know.

Table 4.1 Print Book Scary Terminology – Part 2

Term	Definition
Bleed	Does the print/picture bleed, or run, all the way to the edge of the page, or is there a margin?
BISAC Category	The BISAC category, or Book Industry Standards and Communications Category, are groups the book sellers use to categorize your book. There is a list to choose from.
Key Words	These are the tags that help you to connect with people interested in books like yours. What is your book about? Is it a paranormal 'tween adventure? Is it a mystery with elements of romance? Is it a gothic horror story with space zombies?

First things first. Go to **Createspace.com** (if you've selected that POD company) and create an account. You'll need a user name and password, the usual rigmarole when setting up any online account.

Once you've logged in to your account, you'll be at the **Member Dashboard**. Click Add New Title to start the setup process for your book. Let's walk through the process together.

- What's the **title** of your book? Type it in the space provided.
- Are you publishing a book, audio project or a video project? Select the appropriate button.
- The first time you do this, I recommend the **Guided Step-by-Step Process**. Once you are familiar with the setup (like for your next project) go for the streamlined one-pager.
- Your title will carry over. Who is the primary author of the book? Add that information in as requested.
- **Description**: Take the jacket text that you wrote back in Chapter 2 of this book and copy/paste it to the description section.
- Click on the arrow next to **Add Contributors**. Did you have people helping you who fit any of those categories? If you did, you may want to add contributors.
- Is there a **subtitle** for your book? This is not required but can be helpful in marketing the book later on.
- Is there a **volume number** for this book? Is this the first in a series? You are very likely not to have a volume number, but if you do, type it in the space provided.
- Save and Continue
- Make your **ISBN** selection. Refer back to page 41 if you need information on ISBNs. Don't forget to add the ISBNs to your Front Matter before you PDF. Or PDF again once you've added them.
- Select your **Interior**. Black and White is much cheaper than Full Color. Remember, this selection doesn't impact your cover, just the interior of the book. You can select Black & White and still have a glossy, color cover.
- Select your **Paper Color**. The options are white and cream. The cream is a bit darker than is typical in mass market paperbacks. You might consider ordering a proof copy in each color if you are doing multiple proofs, so that you can make an informed decision. I didn't like the cream and have published all of my books on white paper.

- Change your **Trim Size**. Click on the "Choose a different size" button and select the size you'd like. Remember that your PDF must be formatted for the size you chose. Refer to page 26 for more information on trim sizes.
- **FYI:** the book you are reading now is done on white paper, with a black and white interior and a 6x9 trim size.
- Click **Upload your book file** if you have the formatted, PDF version available.
- Click **Browse** and find your book PDF file on your computer.
- Select the **Bleed** option you want. Remember, bleed is the description for where you want the text/pictures to end on the page, all the way at the edge of the paper, or inside a margin of white space.
- If you check the box next to **Run automated print checks and view formatting issues online**, then you will see what your book will look like when it's printed. This is a good visual check and it will alert you to anything that might hold up your printing. If you have questions about clearing issues, you can call customer service at Createspace and someone can help you.
- **Save.**
- It will take a few minutes for the automated print check to run. Once it has finished, you can **Launch the Interior Reviewer** by clicking the button. Wait another minute or so for it to load.
- **Click Get Started**.
- This brings you to a cool looking virtual book. On the right side of the screen, by the edge of your monitor, there is a column labeled Manuscript Issues. For example, at this very moment, I've uploaded the partial manuscript of this book to help me write this section. One of the issues the **Print Check** alerted me to is an insufficient gutter. The gutter is the inside margin. Books up to 150 pages require a gutter of at least .375 inches. This is something I can correct right now. Sure enough, while the inside

margin was set to .8 inches, the gutter was set to 0. I corrected it in Page Layout, Margins, Custom Margins. I reset the Gutter to .375 for the Whole Document (drop down on the bottom) and it doesn't appear to have made a visible difference in my manuscript, but now it won't be held up on Createspace's end.

- I also have the issue of images less than 300 DPI. Createspace's guidelines state that images less than 300 DPI may be blurry. DPI is an abbreviation for Dots Per Inch. This is a way to measure the digital resolution of a picture. If you don't have the ability to modify your images, you can print the proof as is and see if the pictures come out blurry. I've had this issue come up many times and only once was the image less than I would consider perfect. I asked the illustrator who did the cover art to modify it and I resubmitted the proof.

- Once you've corrected all of your issues, you'll want to upload the corrected document. From the Member Dashboard, click on the title you wish to work on. That will bring you to the **Project Home Page** with all of the setup options. The topics that have been completed will have a green checkmark next to them. The things yet to be done will have a red circle with a white line through them.

Only one thing left to do before you are ready to submit your book for review: Create/Upload your cover.

- From the Project Home Page, click on **Cover**.
- You can: **Build Your Cover Online**, click Professional Cover Design (and pay someone at Createspace to design your cover for you), or Upload a PDF Ready Cover.
- Chances are you want to click Build Your Cover Online, then **Launch Cover Creator**.
- The options that come up are **templates** for the size book you've created. There are LOTS of ways to customize the

templates. There is even an option to upload your pre-formatted cover. Using this option ensures that you get the front, back and spine looking the way you want. For this book, I chose the option with a full picture on the cover and clicked OK.

- This particular cover has six **design elements**: Theme, Front Cover Image, Back Cover Text, Author Photo, Background Color, and Font Color. I'm going to do them out of order.
    - o **Theme**: Try all the options. Every time you click a new option, it applies that theme to the sample text. It might change the colors of the font and background, it might change the font of the text or it might change the sample photo.
    - o **Front Cover Image**: You can use one of Createspace's images for free, but only for books printed through Createspace. It seems that the licensing restrictions would not let you recreate that style for use as an e-book, for example. You might want to call Createspace for more information if you have questions on that. I chose to create my own front cover image in MS PowerPoint, using imagery I purchased from iStockphoto.com. It cost all of $9.99. I saved the MS PowerPoint slide as a .jpg file and uploaded that image.
    - o **Author Photo**: I have a logo that I like to use in lieu of an author photo. I uploaded that image.
    - o **Back Cover Text**: I copied the jacket text that I had written a few days ago and pasted it in the box. I played around with the line spacing on the bullets.
    - o A note about back cover text: I didn't like the way the very wordy text for this book looked in the Createspace template, so I created a back cover in MS Powerpoint and saved it as a jpg file. The text got very fuzzy. It had to do with rastering vs.

vectoring – an artist explained it to me. At any rate, jpg isn't an ideal format if you have lots of text.

- o **Background Color**: I selected a color from the palette that I thought looked nice.
- o **Font Color**: I decided to go with black text to match the front cover image.

- I **submitted the cover**, after reading the directions about size. The cover needs to be just a bit bigger than the book. I had to resize my .jpg from 6x9 to 6.25x9.5 per the directions. It took thirty seconds. You do not necessarily need to spend big bucks on an illustrator to create your cover. If you want something relatively straightforward, try doing it yourself. You might be surprised.

- Click **Continue** after your cover has been submitted. You are now at the Complete Setup section. If you are ready to, you can **Submit Files for Review**.

- The Createspace team will send you an email at some point in the next forty-eight hours to let you know your next steps. They may ask you to correct something. If you don't understand what they've requested, **call them**. They will explain in greater detail. To contact them:
    - o From whatever Createspace screen you are on, click **Help** in the top right corner, next to **Cart**.
    - o On the bottom of the left-side box there is a gray button labeled **Contact Support**. Click it.
    - o On the next screen, there's a box on the right side with a phone receiver on it. Click the **Call Me** button in that box.
    - o Plug in your phone number and they will call you almost immediately. You can schedule the call for a few minutes out, if that works better.

- If you are not ready to submit yet, don't. All of your work to date will be saved. When you are ready, come back and submit your files. For example, I completed the setup while I was writing this section (to be sure the section was correct) but of course, I'm not ready to submit the file for review. I still have five more chapters to write. A few weeks from now, when the manuscript is complete, all I'll have to do is select DIY Publishing from my list of titles on the Member Dashboard, upload a new manuscript document and then submit.

After the Createspace team has reviewed your submission (they are just making sure it meets the print requirements – they print what you send; they don't do any editorial work), they will let you know that you can order your proof copy.

Save yourself hours of hair pulling. **RESIST THE URGE TO BEGIN WORKING ON YOUR DIGITAL EDITION UNTIL AFTER YOU HAVE REVIEWED YOUR PROOF COPY AND FINALIZED YOUR PRINT BOOK.** I can't say this enough. Sometimes in life, it really is best to learn from mistakes other people make.

Wondering what to do whilst you are waiting for that fantabulous proof to arrive? Flip the page, dear author. Flip the page.

Chapter 5:

Storm your Brain & Map your Mind

It's never too early to begin thinking about what you are going to do with your book once it's available to the world. I'm sorry to tell you that the odds of people randomly finding it on their own and filling your PayPal account with millions of dollars is...um...pretty unlikely. Unless you are experienced in marketing, and even if you are, you probably want to spend a little time doing some research.

Jennifer Fusco is a marketing guru who runs a business called Market or Die Author Services. Google "Market or Die" and you'll find her. I recently asked her, "What is the most important thing an author can do to market his/her books?"

Jennifer said, "I think the single thing an author can do, at a minimum, is embrace social media. Social media sells books. It's the fastest way to spread positive word of mouth about you and your work. Some authors are hesitant about engaging in Facebook, Twitter, Goodreads and others. I know it can be a time-suck. However, it's a medium that is beneficial for anyone who has a limited marketing budget and still wants to make some serious cash."

Take it from Fusco the Guru: one aspect of your marketing plan should include a social media campaign. There is plenty of good information out there – take a bit of time while you are waiting for your proof copy to arrive and learn about it.

Now that you've done a bit of reading up on the topic, let's take a look at some specific steps you can take. I like to start with some questions for you to answer. There are no wrong answers to these questions. It doesn't matter how other people would sell their book. How do *you* want to sell *your* book?

1. What are your goals for this project?

Great – your book is, for all intents and purposes, published. A printed, bound copy is on its way to you this very minute (if you've completed Chapter 4). Soon, it will be available to the world. How do you want to handle that?

You need to have a goal (at least one) and you need to write it down.

They (you know them, right?) say that a goal that is written down is much more likely to be achieved than a goal that isn't written down. That makes some sense when you think about it. To write it down, the goal has to be fixed in your mind. It needs substance. If you never write it down, the goal can live in your mind as some kind of nebulous, non-specific idea. It's hard to achieve an idea.

So, what is your goal?

- Was it finalizing the book and having a few copies printed to give as gifts to friends and family? Excellent! You are nearly there.
- Was it to publish a book and be able to say you are an author? Nice job, you did it. Both of these are worthy goals.
- Do you hope to sell the book to a small audience within your community? This could be a physical community or a virtual one.
- Do you hope to sell enough copies to recoup any expenses you might have had in its publication?
- Do you hope to make some significant money with this book?
- Do you hope to make writing a career and want to take the literary world by storm with your debut novel?

Think about this for a couple of days if necessary. Let the idea of a goal marinate in your mind as you go about your normal life.

Remember, there is no goal too outlandish for you to write down in the privacy of your own home.

Brainstorming & Mind Mapping your way to a Marketing Plan

Now that you have a goal, you need a plan for achieving it. Unless you are a marketing expert, writing a marketing plan can be more daunting than writing your book. I'm going to share with you the tools I like to use to create my marketing plan.

Brainstorming and mind mapping. Yup, it's that simple. Okay, well, it's not simple at all, but let's take them one at a time.

You are going to brainstorm answers to a bunch of additional questions. Do them one at a time and not necessarily all in the same sitting. If you are feeling empty of ideas, come back to it tomorrow.

- Start with a blank sheet of paper.
- Write the question out across the top.
- Set a timer for five minutes (I often use the oven timer for things like this.)
- Jot down any answer you can think of to the question.

Don't edit yourself. You are brainstorming here – there is no such thing as a silly answer in a brainstorm. Sometimes practical options come from ridiculous ideas.

If you can't come up with enough ideas, invite some friends over, ply them with a nice bottle of wine and pump them for ideas. Make a game of it.

I've started the list below with question number two, because you've already answered the first and most important question: What is your goal? Here are questions two through six:

2. What kind of people might be interested in reading/buying your book?

3. Where do you find these people?
4. How do those people find books?
5. What images/words/phrases might these people use in a search on the Internet to find a book like yours?
6. What are you willing to do to sell your books?

Example 5.1: Brainstorming

> **What kind of people might be interested in reading/buying** *The Cordovan Vault*
>
> Kids in 4th - 8th grade
> Parents of those kids
> People who give kids gifts
> Adults who like YA books
> Adult adventure story fans
> Adults who like quest stories
> Fans of paranormal stories
> Libraries: public or school
> School PTOs
> School Reading Coordinators

I took a few minutes and thought up this list. Most of the people on the list seem pretty straightforward, but PTOs (Parent/Teacher Organizations) seems like a strange place to try and find buyers for my book. The idea popped into my head because I'm on a PTO and I have PTO duties nagging at my brain at this moment. But I left it on the list, because you never know...maybe I could get in front of some PTOs and do an assembly at a school or something. At any rate, now isn't the time for editing, now is the time for creative thinking. I thought PTO, so I put it on the list.

Once you have brainstormed ideas to answer questions 2-6, you are going to create a mind map to organize those ideas.

If you Google mind map, you get a lot of different definitions, but the definition I like best is from Wikipedia: *a diagram of ideas around a central theme.* You are going to need another blank piece of paper.

I like to draw my mind maps on a big piece of paper oriented in a landscape fashion. I often pull off a big (kid's table sized) piece of my kids' roll of art paper and write my mind map on it so that there is plenty of space. But to conform to the boundaries of this book, here's an idea of what a mind map might look like.

Example 5.2: Basic Mind Map

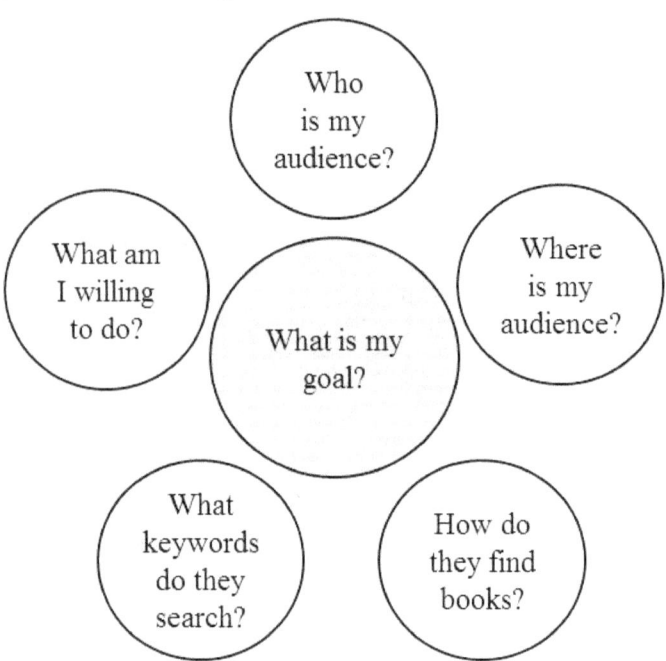

Plug your answers to the questions into the circles. If you have any really crazy, outlandish ideas from your brainstorming that you would never in a million years actually do, you can edit them out now.

Of course, you can (and should) add any additional question(s) that you think apply to your book and your situation. Certainly, these are not the only considerations.

If you want to do this online (some folks think better with a keyboard in front of them) you can Google "free mind mapping online" and end up at a bunch of applications to choose from.

Here's a mind map I created for *The Cordovan Vault* to give you an idea of how it could look.

Example 5.3: Mind Map for The Cordovan Vault

Now that I've organized my marketing ideas, I can use them to create a plan to achieve my goal.

I have a nice, specific, measurable goal. I'd like to sell five hundred copies of *The Cordovan Vault* in 2014. Using ideas from my mind map, I'll think of actions I can take to achieve that goal. Here's a sample marketing plan:

Example 5.4: Sample Marketing Plan

Who is the audience? Who's buying the book?

- Get the book in front of kids in grades 4-8.
  - o Have a booth at a kid-centric event.

- o Be a guest at a school where kids might buy a signed book.
- o Create buzz on the Internet where kids might see it.
- o Make the book attractive to kids with e-readers.
- Get in front of Parents
- o Find parent blogs and attempt to become a guest.
- o Find parent groups and be a guest speaker.
- o Find grandparent blogs and attempt to be a guest.
- o Have a booth in an office building around a gift giving time/summer reading time.
- Get in front of YA readers
- o Find a YA-Con type of conference that readers attend.
- o Find book fairs and have a booth.
- o Be a guest speaker at a library.
- o Buy an advertisement on Kindle Nation.

I've now drawn up a list of twelve ideas of things I can do to make progress toward achieving my goal. With enough time, I'm sure I could come up with a hundred more. But those are specific, actionable things I can (and will!) do. It's a plan to market my book.

Your marketing plan doesn't need to be fancy in order to be workable. Over time, you'll learn what things are effective and what things don't work.

Spend a little time, while you are waiting for your proof copy to arrive, and create a marketing plan that will help you meet your goals. One fun thing here: you are only limited by your imagination.

Chapter 6: Finalize Your Print Book

Has UPS arrived with a little package for you? Open it up. Are you holding your book in your hand? Yipppppeeeeee! Smell it. Pet it. This is your moment...revel in it! Happy dance if you are moved to do so. This is a BIG accomplishment. For many of you, like me, it is a moment that you have dreamed of your whole life. Take a mental picture so you can remember it forever.

Click.

All right, that's done, now let's get back to work. Get yourself a pen – in a color that you can easily see on the page – red, blue, pink, purple, whatever – and make yourself comfortable. You need to look at the book and mark any changes you want to make.

- I write my notes about the front cover on the inside of it, and about the back cover on the inside of that.
- How does the cover look? Is it everything you had hoped it would be?
- How about the back cover? Are there any layout issues to be fixed or (God forbid!) typos?
- Double check your headers and footers all the way through. Do they line up correctly?
- Does the font look nice? Easy to read, professional looking? Consistent throughout the book?
- Are your chapter headings the same style throughout the book?
- Does your Table of Contents match the chapter titles, pages numbers, etc?
- How do your pictures look? Are they clear or are they blurry and pixelated?

Now you need to read the book, every word, as if this is the first time you are seeing it. It's hard to do when you've already been through the manuscript a zillion times. At least it's in a new and exciting format. That often helps me get through it.

Mark all of the changes you want to make in your proof copy because you might want to refer back to that proof when you get your next proof.

After you've noted any flaws or issues in your proof, you need to go back to your manuscript and input those changes and save your document. I like to save it as *xyz book v2.doc* so that I still have the original in case something should happen.

 One thing I haven't written about, but which is **CRITICALLY** important is backing up your work. You need to have a backup copy saved someplace other than your hard drive. You never know what might happen to your computer and you don't want to lose all your hard work.

For a cheap and easy (free) backup, I like to email the file to myself as an attachment and save it in a folder in my email. That way it's saved on Gmail's servers as well as on my laptop.

- Once you have input all of your changes to your manuscript, PDF it again.
- Open Createspace.com and log into your account.
- From your Member Dashboard, click on the title of your book.
- This will bring you to the Project Homepage. Each of the steps you took to create your proof are summarized here.
- To upload your new document, click on Interior and give it a minute to load. You should see a little wheel spinning next to the page name on the tab in your browser.
- You can make changes to your book's interior in this section. If you want to upload a new copy of your book, click the link "Upload a different file." You will get a warning that informs you that making changes to your interior will overwrite your existing file.
- It will need to be reviewed, again, by Createspace.com.

Order another proof copy and go through this process as many times as it takes until you feel you have produced the very best book you can.

Now that you have a perfect print book, you can launch your book if you don't plan to have a digital version. If you want to make it available digitally, too, then now is the time to open up your latest version of the print book and make an e-book copy. Make sure it's a separate version. You are going to make LOTS of changes; in fact, you are going to undo a lot of the work you did to make the print version.

Chapter 7:

Formatting Matters: Digital Books

Now that your print book is finalized, you can begin thinking about your digital version. One of the biggest mistakes I made the first time I Indie Published was that I made the digital version first. When I got my print proof copy, I found that there were changes to be made. Finding the same places in the digital, page-number-less version was a pain in the patootie. It made LOTS of extra work for me.

About E-Books

While the text of your manuscript is the same, e-books, or digital books, are different from print books in a couple of fundamental ways. For one thing, the concept of pages is gone. Because the e-reader device allows the person reading the book to modify the size of the font for the comfort of their eyes, you (the author) have no way of knowing how much writing will appear on the screen at one time. Therefore, no pages.

For another thing, margins, headers, and footers don't apply. Tables and charts may not look the way you expect, because of the changes to font size. It may not seem like much of a difference, but it has broad implications to the way you layout your book.

Formatting your E-Book

The first thing you will want to do is to open up the latest version of your print document and save a copy with a new file name. Something like *The World's Best Book Ever digital book v1.doc*.

Next, decide which tool you will use to digitally publish. Table 7.1 compares a couple of popular options.

Table 7.1 DIY Digital Publication Tools

Website	Pro's & Con's
Smashwords.com	Smashwords is a fabulous, author-driven site that allows you to digitally publish your book. It's free to publish and a very user-friendly community. You can choose to have Smashwords send your book to many other vendors automatically, including Sony, Baker & Taylor, Kobo, Apple, Amazon*, Diesel, Barnes & Noble. I love Smashwords. You can create coupon codes to give discounts if you'd like. Lots of stuff is available for free, or $.99. It's a great site. The only drawback (and it's not a big deal, but something to consider) is that for people to purchase your book on Smashwords (not the other distribution channels they do for you) people buy it on their computer and then drag and drop the file that they've downloaded to their e-reader. It's an additional step in the purchase process but for users who are used to buying from Amazon for Kindle, for example. * Smashwords is still working out the technical kinks of sending to Amazon. At the moment, only books that have sold at least $2,000 are being considered.

Website	Pro's & Con's
Amazon's Kindle Direct	You can digitally publish your book directly on Amazon through Kindle Direct. It's free to use and pretty easy. One thing to note: unlike Smashwords, publishing on AKD will only make your book available on Amazon, but buyers can use the Kindle Whispersync technology to buy it for delivery directly on the Kindle. Another consideration: some authors choose to make their e-book exclusively available on Amazon. This might improve their Amazon ranking since people can only buy the book from Amazon, but then Nook readers can't get a digital copy. It's something for you to consider when developing your marketing plan. Do some research on it, there are a lot of authors out there talking about their experiences with AKD – both good and bad. You need to decide what is right for you and your book.
Barnes & Noble's Nook Press	Nook Press is Barnes & Noble's answer to Kindle Direct. It's very easy to use and allows Nook users to buy and load your book directly to their device. Smashwords does currently upload to Barnes & Noble.com daily.

Now that you've selected which tool to use you will need to follow the formatting guidelines for each tool.

Formatting for Smashwords

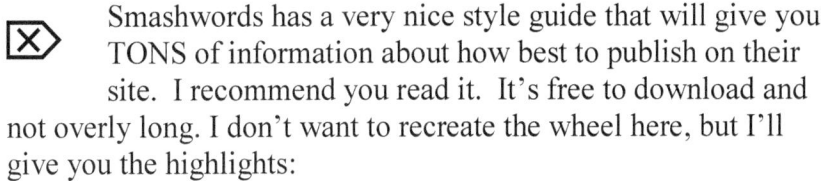 Smashwords has a very nice style guide that will give you TONS of information about how best to publish on their site. I recommend you read it. It's free to download and not overly long. I don't want to recreate the wheel here, but I'll give you the highlights:

- The first thing you need to do is to get rid of all the crazy, hidden formatting taggies that MS Word automatically puts into your document without you knowing. Smashwords says that skipping this step is most often the source of problems when uploading to their site. There's an easy way to do it.

- Copy and paste your entire document to Notepad to remove all those taggies. Notepad is a text editor that comes as part of Windows. To find it, click on your Windows icon, then select all programs and scroll to Accessories. Notepad is in that folder (usually.)

- Copy/paste it, again, from **Notepad** to a <u>new</u> word processing document. This reformats your document to the very basics – pulling out all that annoying, problematic stuff that you didn't know was there.

- Activate Show/Hide – the big backward P or the ¶ symbol. This shows you all of the formatting – spaces and everything else embedded in your document. See page 26 for more information on how to do this.

- Turn off Autocorrect and Autoformat in MS Word. As I'm sure you know, MS Word often thinks it knows what you want better than you do and getting it to stop "helping" can be a challenge. To turn it off in MS Word 2010, click File, Help, Options, Proofing, Autocorrect Options, and then click the Autocorrect, Autoformat and Autoformat As You Type tabs. On each tab, you will need to uncheck the checked boxes. Click "OK" after you've changed all three tabs.

- Normalize all of your text styles. MS Word has a bunch of styles – Normal, Heading 1, Title and so forth. They all look different. You can modify those styles and use them to your advantage.
  - o I usually delete all but a couple of them. I keep Normal (for regular text), Title (for the title page) and Heading 1 (for chapter headings).
  - o To modify these in MS Word, click on the little down arrow in the Styles box on the Home tab. Rest the mouse on the style you want to modify and a drop down arrow appears on the right. Click it and select Modify.
  - o If the changes you want to make aren't options in the box that opens up, click Format (down on the bottom left) and you can change just about everything in one of those choices: font, paragraph, etc.
- Work your way back through the manuscript and add some of your formatting in again. Not page numbers, headers, footers or things like that. But you want to be sure your text looks the way you want it to look. Bolded things need to be re-bolded. Fix your italics, if you had any. Things like that.
- If you want the first word of each paragraph indented, add that to your Normal style – don't use tabs.
- Be sure you have the ¶ symbol at the end of your paragraphs, not ↵.
- Don't use section breaks in your e-book formatting. Use page breaks instead (*Insert, Page Break.*) Remember, you only needed section breaks in your print book in order to put in your headers and footers. Your digital version won't have those.
- Read about the Smashwords Premium Catalog. This is how you get your book onto Barnes & Noble and all of

the other sites. You will need a new ISBN for your e-version. Get a free one from Smashwords.

- Don't forget to modify your front matter appropriately. Smashwords does have some recommended language that is specific to e-books.
- If you want to have one, you can make a hyperlinked Table of Contents to allow your reader to jump from chapter to chapter with a click.
    - o There are several ways to do this and in fact, MS Word will do it for you since you've used the styles, but I never like how it comes out. Take a look for yourself. Click the page where you want your TOC to be. Click the References tab, click the drop down next to Table of Contents and select the style you want.
    - o To create a hyperlinked TOC manually, type it up. Highlight the first chapter name in the TOC and right click. Choose Hyperlink and then click Bookmark. You'll see your book in outline format. Scroll to the point you want the hyperlink to take the reader to and click OK. Do this for the entire TOC.
- You can also link to other books, websites, etc.
- Remember that digital book audiences can modify the font size on their e-reader. Limit the number of different fonts you use. Smashwords recommends that you don't use any fonts bigger than 14.
- If you have pictures in the manuscript, you'll need to embed them. Smashwords won't allow floating pictures. If you copied and pasted pictures into your manuscript, you need to delete those and insert the pictures.
    - o Save the pictures in a file on your computer.
    - o Go to the place in the document where you want a picture.
    - o Click *Insert, Picture, Browse* for the picture you want and click *OK*.

- You may need to modify the size of the picture or otherwise reformat it. Right click on the picture and choose Format Picture. There are a TON of options in this area, including crop and color modifications.
- Right click on the picture and you can select Wrap Text to tell the text where to appear in reference to the picture. I often use "Tight" and then drag and drop my picture to where I want it. It's still embedded.
- You will need to modify your cover image. The print-book cover image you made had a front, a spine and a back. The image for your e-book is just a front – usually in a "book" shape, or vertical rectangle.
  - Smashwords came out with new book cover guidelines last year. Apple requires that the minimum size for covers be 1400 pixels wide.
  - Smashwords recommends that the art be 1600 pixels by 2400 pixels.
  - They do have a list of inexpensive cover artists they can recommend if you need help and don't know where else to turn.

Publishing on Smashwords

Now that you've reformatted your manuscript and cover art, you are ready to upload to Smashwords.

- Create an account on Smashwords.com with a user name and password.
- Click Publish.
  1. Type in your **title and synopsis**. There is space for a short synopsis and a longer synopsis. You may have to modify your jacket text to fit the short synopsis section as it's limited to 400 characters.

Select the language that your book is written in and click the applicable radio button regarding the adult-ness of the content.

2. Make a **pricing & sampling** decision. Do you want your book to be free, cost whatever the reader feels like paying or a set price? You can change the price of the book later, if you'd like.

    Deciding on price can be tricky. For non-fiction, pricing too low can be an indicator to readers that you don't know what you are talking about. Conversely, price your book too high and nobody will buy it because it's too expensive. Do some research into what similar books cost.

    For fiction, there's been a rush of $.99 e-books out there. Dean Wesley Smith wrote a lot of articles (September 2012) about price that are sure worth a look. I'm way generalizing here, but basically he's saying that traditional publishers have been telling buyers that e-books are cheap at $9.99 to the point where people are beginning to believe them.

    He says that we Indie Publishers should bring our prices up a bit but stay under that range. I think the idea here is that the $.99 e-book craze reduces the perceived value of our work and is actually hurting us in the long run.

    Conversely, Mark Coker founder of Smashwords, predicts the traditional publishers will reduce their prices on e-books this year, to under the $4.00 mark.

    Certainly, price is an important factor and something that you should give weighty consideration to.

How much of your book would you like to give away as a free sample? People often read a sample before deciding to purchase the book and it's a good idea. Smashwords defaults to 20% for a sample, but you can modify that if you'd like.

3. How would you **categorize** your book? Follow the drop down (well – to the side) arrows to make a selection. This is how people will find it, so pick the category that makes the most sense.
4. Add **tags** to further help people find your book. These are keywords that people who'd like to read your book might search.
5. Unclick the boxes next to any **e-book formats** that you don't want your book available in. Does that make sense? Smashwords defaults to all available formats, but you don't have to use them all. I'm not sure why you wouldn't, but it's up to you.
6. Browse for your new e-book **cover image** and add it.
7. Browse for your new Smashwords **manuscript file** and add it here.
8. Read the **publishing agreement** and click publish.

The first time I published with Smashwords, it took hours for the file to upload. I was something like 1,267 in the queue, but it uploaded fine. I don't remember it being so long after that. Don't worry if it takes a while.

Formatting for Amazon Kindle Direct (AKD)

When I made a version of *The Peacock Tale* for AKD, I used the Smashwords file on my computer as a starting place. Again, I made a copy and named it something like *The Peacock Tale kindle version*. I know; I'm terribly clever that way. I made some changes to the front matter, removing any references to Smashwords and noting that this was the Amazon Kindle version.

The only real difference I noted as I published with AKD was that for some reason, when I put it up on Amazon, the indentation at the beginning of each paragraph (from the normal style) didn't hold up. It wasn't there and I didn't like the way the text looked. I tried adding a tab at the beginning of the paragraphs and that didn't work either. In the end, I added a 6pt space after each paragraph (under Formatting, Paragraphs) and while there's no indenting, at least there's a visual break between the paragraphs.

Publishing on AKD

To put a book up on Amazon through Kindle Direct (AKD) you need to have an Amazon account. Go to KDP.Amazon.com. I had trouble making the web address work, so I went to Google and typed in Amazon Kindle Direct and got a link. It brought me to a sign in page. From there, click Add Title and follow the step by step directions.

1. **Enter your book details** – Title, part of a series, edition, description (copy and paste the jacket text you wrote earlier), contributors, language, publication date, publisher (it's you) and ISBN.

    Remember your Createspace ISBN is only good for your print book and your Smashwords ISBN is only good for your Smashwords version. Since Amazon doesn't *require* an ISBN for your AKD version, I didn't bother to buy a new one, but I did remove the Smashwords ISBN from the front matter.

2. **Verify your publication rights** – since we've already established that you are publishing something that is your "original work," not something written by anyone else, you can check the box stating that it is not a public domain work. If you are unsure about who the copyright holder is for the work you are publishing, you should seek advice from an attorney.

3. **Target your book to customers** – add categories and keywords. These are places where, or ideas, someone might search if they were looking for a book like yours.

   For example, for *The Cordovan Vault*, I might choose the **category** Juvenile Fiction, subcategory Action/Adventure, subcategory General. You can follow the drop down trail by clicking on the + sign next to the topics.

   As **keywords** for *The Cordovan Vault*, I might choose 'tween paranormal adventure, quest, middle grade adventure and other things like that, up to the limit of seven. Separate your keyword phrases with a comma and each *phrase* counts as one keyword.

4. **Upload your book cover** – click Browse and upload your cover.

5. **Upload your book file** – before you can upload your file, you need to make a DRM selection. DRM stands for Digital Rights Management. Wikipedia has a lot of information about DRM and is a good source for you.

   I can't advise you on the question of DRM because, honestly, I don't understand it well enough. I can tell you what I do. I choose "no" for encryption because I'm not convinced it actually helps prevent plagiarism. I'm of the opinion that if somebody wants to plagiarize me, they will find a way to do it, DRM or no, and some people make the argument that active DRM can make it more difficult for legitimate customers to access my books.

   Once you decide which way to go, click the applicable radio button. Browse for your book file and upload it.

6. **Preview your book** – click the previewer and flip through your book to see how it looks.

7. **Verify your publishing territories** – since we've already established that you are publishing something that is your "original work" not something written by anyone else,

you have the worldwide rights to publish. If you are unsure about the type of rights you hold for the work you are publishing, you should seek advice from an attorney.

8. **Choose your royalty rate** – this is the percentage you get for each copy sold. Click the 35% and 70% radio buttons and see the information that populates in the chart. These rates are a guide to help you set your pricing.

See page 70 for information on pricing.

9. **Kindle book lending** – this is the place where you decide if you'll allow people who've bought your book to lend it to others. I'm a fan of this option. I'd like as many people to read my book as possible in the hopes that they will like it and buy others. But again, this option is up to you.

When you have completed all the sections, click the acknowledgement box (after you've read the blurb, of course) to the left and above the **Save and Publish** button, then click the button.

Formatting for Nook Press and other sites

To get your book up on Barnes & Noble's website right away, you can publish it directly for the Nook through Nook Press. The process is very similar to the Amazon process. By this point, you are enough of an expert to make your way through.

Woot-woot! You are now a published author! Nice job. Once you have your books available for sale, and sometimes it takes a couple of days for everything to filter around the internet, you can start marketing. How you ask? See Chapter 8 to get started.

Chapter 8: Marketing

Fabulouso! You are a published author with products to sell. Excellent. Now what do you do?

First, you need to launch your book. You can throw yourself a party, inviting your friends and family to celebrate the achievement of a lifelong dream. And you can contact people you know who might be willing and able to help you get the word out about your new product.

Next, dust off that marketing plan you drew up a while back (chapter 5). You had some great ideas there. Start putting those ideas into action.

If you want this little business to take off there are some things that authors commonly do to connect with their audience. You might try doing some (or all) of these things:

- **Create a website for yourself** – I created one for free through Google. You can see it at www.jmonkeys.com. It's not the best in the world, but it'll do until I make enough money to hire someone to do it for me.
- **Create a blog** – a blog is place where you can write short, interactive (people get the chance to comment) blurbs about an idea. I'm part of a group blog on the topic of writing: Writing Secrets of 7 Scribes (secretsof7scribes.wordpress.com). I'm Saturday's Scribe. Wordpress and Blogger are two common blog hosting sites. Wordpress is free; Blogger is too.
- **Create a Facebook page** – J Monkeys has a Facebook page, in addition to my personal FB page. I haven't done as much with J's page as I likely should have so far, but hey it's a big job. Since I was thinking about it, I just posted a little comment about my progress writing this book. If you *like* my page over at facebook.com/AuthorJMonkeys, you can see my witty comments and keep abreast of my progress on my next project.

- **Create a newsletter** – perhaps twice a year send a note about your work and upcoming books to folks who've opted in. At every event you do you'll want to collect people's email addresses to add to your list – with their permission, of course. Mailchimp is one free service that will help you with newsletter management. I haven't started using it yet myself, but it's the next thing on my marketing to do list after I finish this book. Go *like* me on Facebook or check out my website to find out more about my newsletter adventures.
- **Book Trailer** – you can create a book trailer or other video and put it up on YouTube. I've just started doing this. My YouTube channel (http://www.youtube.com/user/jmonkeywriter/videos) has just one video on it right now, but I recently created a new video (using MS PowerPoint!) for Dixie & Taco which I'll be modifying and posting up there soon.
- **Twitter** – ugh, Twitter. Yes, I have a Twitter account, but I'm not a very good tweeter. I'm a novelist, not a short story writer. I don't think in 140 character sound-bites. I'll have to get better at this. I'm @JMonkeys1 on Twitter, if you want to follow me. I'll be tackling Twitter later this year, too.
- **Lectures** – you might consider developing a lecture or class on a topic that seems appropriate to what you write and try to get speaking engagements. There is often an opportunity to sell your books at those types of events. I'll let you in on a little secret: that's why I decided to write this book...to share my experiences Indie Publishing with other folks who might like to do it but don't know where to start.
- **Media** – don't forget to share your accomplishments with your local media. You never know where something might take you.

One thing to remember here is this: Pace yourself. Rome wasn't built in a day; neither will you have all of these things in place and steaming along in a short time. Each of these things can be simple and terribly frustrating at the same time. It took longer for me to create my JMonkeys Facebook page than it did to create my website on Google. I had only a tiny bit of web creation experience and was way more comfortable with Facebook, but there it was.

Another thing to think about is to occasionally remember to pat yourself on the back for all the things you *have* accomplished rather than berate yourself for those things you haven't gotten to yet.

Three years ago, I hadn't published a thing and I was ready to give up the dream of being a published author. Today, I have eight books available and counting. I have a social media presence (FB, Twitter, Web, Blog). I have other products for sale (plush that coordinates with my picture books) and I have a TON of ideas for what comes next.

So don't sweat it if you don't meet your goals right away. This isn't an instant gratification business. Take your time and enjoy the journey.

Chapter 9: Being a Small Business Owner

Hey, guess what? If you plan to continue writing and selling books, you have just become a small business owner.

Congratulations!

Owning your own business means a lot of different things. This certainly isn't an exhaustive list, but here are some of the things that I've come across.

- You will likely need a bank account specifically for your business.
- You may want a PayPal account specifically for your business. Many of the businesses that I work with (Createspace, Smashwords, etc.) use PayPal to pay me and I've used PayPal to pay vendors.
- You may want the ability to accept credit card payments. There are a lot of ways to do this. I used to use the old knuckle-buster system from the 1980's. It's low tech, but it's cheap and it works. My bank hooked me up – talk to yours about options. Now I use a little tool called Square that will allow you to use your smartphone or tablet to swipe credit cards for a nominal fee. You can find more information at www.squareup.com.
- You will want to track your business financials carefully. You need to be able to account for the money that you take in and what you spend on the business. I use a series of spreadsheets that I developed myself (DIY!), but there are software packages that you can buy if you'd like.
- Depending on where you live, you may be required to register for a Tax ID to collect, and pay, sales tax.
- You may be required to file business income taxes in addition to your personal income taxes. In Connecticut, where I live, you will probably be required to file quarterly sales and use taxes, too. It's actually pretty straightforward; I've been doing it myself so far.

- You will probably want to have marketing materials made up. I use Vista Print for my promotional supplies. I have business cards, fliers, brochures, notecards (these come in more handy than I would have thought), bookmarks, and a bunch of other things.
- You may want to join a professional organization or two. There are a lot of writing organizations which offer great networking opportunities, conferences, and classes. I'm a member of two (CTRWA & CAPA) and even if I don't attend the meetings very often, I have certainly gotten enough out of them to make my membership dues worthwhile.

Good luck!

Additional Resources

Here are some details on the additional resources I mentioned throughout the book. As a little disclaimer here, I don't get any sort of compensation or kick back from any of these companies, services or websites, I just find them useful..

Topic	Website	Details
Advice on Indie Publishing	Deanwesleysmith.com	Dean Wesley Smith is a bestselling author who has walked away from Traditional Publishing and moved into the Indie Publishing world. He's been doing it for a while and he's got a TON of good practical advice for newbies.
	Thepassivevoice.com	This is a blog written by Passive Guy. PG is an intellectual property rights lawyer and while his blog shouldn't be considered legal advice, he absolutely has an interesting and valuable perspective on Indie Publishing.
Advice on e-books	Thewritersguideto epublishing.com	This blog is also known as the WG2E (Writers Guide 2 E-publishing) and it has a ton of great information on e-publishing specifically.

Topic	Website	Details
Creating Covers and Other Art	istockphoto.com	This is a website where you can buy inexpensive photos to use in your cover art.
	ifreelance.com	This website can connect you with all sorts of artists to do illustrations, cover art, digital work, etc.
Editorial Assistance	crazydiamondediting.word press.com	If you'd like to hire a wonderful freelance editor, feel free to check out my friend Jane Haertel's services.
Copyright Law	Copyright.gov	This is the official site for the US Copyright Office. It has a TON of great information, written so that it's easily understood by laypeople.
	Copyright.gov/Circs/ Circ1.pdf	This is the location for the Basics flyer by the US Copyright Office.
	Mandatory Deposit Address	Publishers are required to deposit two copies of all the books they publish with the Library of Congress. Here's the address: Library of Congress Copyright Office CAD 407 101 Independence Ave SE Washington, DC 20559-6607
ISBNs	Bowker.com	Bowker is an ISBN broker. If you'd like to do so, you can buy ISBNs from Bowker and be the publisher of record for your books.

Topic	Website	Details
Print Companies	Createspace.com	Createspace is a POD or Print on Demand company that will produce bound, print copies of your book for an inexpensive price.
	Lulu.com	Lulu is another POD company. They print a wider range of book sizes than Createspace but are more expensive.
	Printplace.com	PrintPlace.com is a printer of marketing materials, but they print booklets. If you are publishing a short, 4-color picture book and want an inexpensive version – you can order a high quantity from them.
	Vistaprint.com	Vistaprint is another marketing materials print company. They do inexpensive business cards, brochures, flyers and things, but not booklets.
E-Publishing Companies	Smashwords.com	Smashwords is an author driven e-book publishing site. It's free and publishes to many different venues.
	KDP.amazon.com	This is Amazon's Kindle Direct Publishing. Use it to put your e-book on Amazon.
	Nookpress.com	This is Barnes & Noble's direct publishing site. Use it to put your e-book on Barnes & Noble.com.

Topic	Website	Details
Marketing Information	Marketordie.net	Find practical marketing advice/services for authors from Jennifer Fusco.
Social Media	Wordpress.com	According to their own site, "WordPress is a free, Web-based software program that anyone can use to build and maintain a website or blog."
	Blogger.com	Blogger is Google's free tool for creating blogs.
	sites.Google.com	Create your own website on Google for free.
	GoodReads.com	Goodreads is a site for book lovers to talk about, review and rate books.
	Twitter.com	Nearly ubiquitous social media sites to pimp yourself, your thoughts and your books.
	Facebook.com	
Accepting Credit Card Payments	Squareup.com	Square is a credit card reader that works through smartphones and tablets.
	Paypal.com	Paypal is an online company that allows money transfers via the internet.
Newsletter Assistance	Mailchimp.com	Create and email newsletters with this free service.

Topic	Website	Details
Professional Associations	RWA.org	Romance Writers of America is a huge professional organization that advances the interests of romance writers.
	CTRWA.org	CT RWA is the Connecticut chapter of the Romance Writers of America organization. It's a very active chapter with many experienced writers as members.
	authorsandpublishersct.ning.com	CAPA or the Connecticut Authors and Publisher's Association is a large and active professional organization.
About J Monkeys	Jmonkeys.com	J Monkey's website.
	writingsecretsof7scribes.wordpress.com	J Monkey's blog on writing. Enjoy the thoughts of one scribe a day, every day. I'm Saturday's scribe.

Section Checklists

The following pages contain checklists for the sections on Getting Started, Formatting Matters: Print Books, Finalize Your Print Book, and Formatting Matters: Digital Books.

There is a Marketing Idea page in this section and a "To Do List" of common author social networking and marketing

I didn't create checklists for uploading your material to the POD companies nor the e-publishing companies because their processes are set up like a sort of checklist.

These checklists are also available in the DIY Publishing ~ Cheap & Easy Companion Workbook with enough copies for your first five books.

Getting Started Checklist

Step	Done?	Notes To Yourself
Edit the manuscript yourself. • Spellcheck • Find / Replace unnecessary words		
Determine the type of outside **editor** you need. • Content Editor • Copy/Line Editor • Proofreader		
Find an editor & negotiate compensation.		
Input the editor's changes into your manuscript.		
Send the edited manuscript to your **Beta Readers** for input.		
Decide what **Format** you want to publish. • Print Book • Digital Book • Both		
Create **Cover Art** for the appropriate format.		
Write **Jacket Text** for the back of the book.		
Create an **Author Bio**graphy and save it somewhere accessible.		

Formatting Matters ~ Print Books Checklist

Step	Done?	Notes To Yourself
Turn on **Show/Hide**. (aka The Big Backward P)		
Decide on the best **Size** for your book.		
Mirror your **Margins** with the inside margin larger than the outside. • Add a blank page at the beginning to see the "real" layout.		
Change all of your page breaks to **Section Breaks**.		
Create your **Headers and Footers** • Add page numbers.		
Consider adding your **Copyright Notice.**		
Add the **"Dude, don't sue me"** statement.		
Add your **ISBN**.		
Add other **Contributors**.		
Add a **Dedication** or **Acknowledgement**.		
Add a **Table of Contents,** if appropriate.		
Put some **Advertising** information at the end of the book.		

Formatting Matters ~ Print Books Checklist (continued)

Step	Done?	Notes To Yourself
Review your Document to be sure everything is just how you want it. • Are your paragraphs visually appealing? • Do your margins make sense?		
Delete that blank page at the beginning, if you added one.		
PDF the document.		
Upload the pdf to your POD company.		
Once it's passed the POD company review, order your **Proof Copy**.		

Finalize Your Print Book Checklist

Step	Done?	Notes To Yourself
Receive your **Proof Copy**. Smell it. Pet it. Love it.		
Carefully review the **Front** and **Back Covers**. Note changes on the inside.		
When you open the book, is the **Title Page** the first thing you see? Is it on the right?		
Is the **Copyright Info** on the back side of the title page, on the left? Read it. Any typos?		
Does your **Font** look nice? Is it easy to read?		
Is your **Table of Contents** lined up properly?		
Do the **Page Numbers** for each chapter on the TOC match the page number at the start of each chapter?		
Flip through the entire book page by page looking at the **Headers and Footers**. Are they the way you want them to look?		
Do you have **Pictures**? Look at each one and evaluate its pixelated-ness.		
Read every word. Are their errors that need fixing?		

Finalize Your Print Book Checklist (continued)

Step	Done?	Notes To Yourself
Input the necessary changes in your new document.		
PDF the document.		
Re-upload the pdf to your POD company.		
Once it's passed the POD company review, order your **Second Proof Copy.**		
Repeat this process as many times as necessary until you are convinced your book is as perfect as it can be. I usually have **three** proofs.		

Formatting Matters ~ Digital Books Checklist

Step	Done?	Notes To Yourself
Save a copy of your final print book to prepare as your e-book.		
Decide on your e-book **Publisher**. • Smashwords • AKD • Nook Press • All of the above		
Read the Smashwords formatting style guide, if appropriate.		
Create the taggie-free version using Notepad.		
Activate **Show/Hide**.		
Turn off **Autocorrect**.		
Normalize your text styles.		
Re-format. • Limit the variety of font sizes. • Add bold. • Fix italics. • Remove page numbers, headers and footers. • Remove tabs. Indent through Normal Style.		
Verify that paragraphs end with ¶ not ↵.		

Formatting Matters ~ Digital Books Checklist (continued)

Step	Done?	Notes To Yourself
Remove Section Breaks. **Use** page breaks as necessary.		
Get a new **ISBN** for your e-book version or remove the print book number.		
Change your **Front Matter** to reflect the e-book version.		
Make a hyperlinked **TOC**.		
Add any **Other Hyperlinks** you'd like.		
Embed **Pictures**.		
Save and prepare to **Upload** your work to the e-publisher of your choice.		
Modify your **Cover** image.		
Create versions for **AKD** and **Nook Press** as needed.		

Marketing Brainstorm Idea Sheet

1.   What is your goal?

2.   What kind of people might be interested in reading/buying
      your book?

3.   Where do you find these people?

4.   How do those people find books?

5.   What images/words/phrases might these people use in a
      search on the Internet to find a book like yours?

6.   What are you willing to do to sell your books?

7.   What else should you be thinking about?

Common Author Marketing To Do List

Create a **Website** for yourself.

Create a **Blog** for yourself (this can also be your website – you may or may not want both.)

Create an author **Facebook** page.

Create a **Twitter** account.

Create a **Book Trailer**.

Create a **Newsletter** (perhaps twice a year, but at every event you do you'll want to collect people's email addresses to add to your list – with their permission, of course.)

Use the **Media** whenever possible. If you've got an event coming up or a new book coming out, inform your local media.

Create a **Lecture** that you can offer to the right folks. This gives you a chance to get in front of them and talk about you and your work.

About J Monkeys

J Monkeys has always been a storyteller, although mostly just for self-entertainment. J was shocked to learn that everybody didn't spend their time with their head in a cloud imagining what they would do if some kind of adventure presented itself. After getting a degree in Creative Writing from the University of Connecticut (Go Huskies!) and spending WAY too long writing boring things for a regular paycheck, J first Indie Published in March 2011. Since then, J's popped out eight Indie books, including the latest project: *DIY Publishing ~ Cheap & Easy*.

J lives in Connecticut with a menagerie of children and pets and is hard at work on the next project. See www.jmonkeys.com for more details.

Books by J Monkeys:

In the Woods
Dixie & Taco go to Grandmother's House
Dixie & Taco go to Grandmother's House (English & Spanish)
Dixie & Taco go to the Zoo
Dixie & Taco go to the Beach
Brook the Fish
The Cordovan Vault
The Peacock Tale
DIY Publishing ~ Cheap & Easy
DIY Publishing ~ Cheap & Easy – Companion Workbook

Coming Attractions:
Street Sign Scavenger Hunt (in February 2014)
Gastric-Genealogy (my family history cookbook – due in 2014)
Gastric-Genealogy Template (DIY family cookbook due in 2014)